Empowerment

Through
Mastering Anxiety

&

Finding Your
Assertive Voice

Ken Welburn, Ph.D., C. Psych.

Mountaintop Alchemy Publishers
M.A.P. Publishers, 2015

Library and Archives Canada Cataloguing in Publication

Welburn, Ken, 1952-, author
Empowerment through mastering anxiety & finding your assertive
voice / Dr. Ken Welburn.

Includes bibliographical references and index.
ISBN 978-0-9880109-0-1 (pbk.)

1. Self-actualization (Psychology). 2. Anxiety. 3. Assertiveness
(Psychology). I. Title.

BF637.S4W34 2014   158.1   C2014-907065-9

Typeset in *Sabon* at SpicaBookDesign
Printed in Canada by Printorium Bookworks / Island Blue, Victoria B.C.

For Yolande

Acknowledgements

I acknowledge my deepest gratitude and appreciation to my wife, Yolande Lamothe, who graciously and competently serves as both my editor and my muse. Your diligent editing always challenges me to do better. Our animated conversations gave birth to this book and you have been a cornerstone in its development from the original concept to the printing of these pages. Your loyalty and support are my haven.

My exposure to assertiveness training began as soon as I entered the doctoral program at the University of Ottawa in 1983. I had the good fortune to be mentored in assertiveness training by two psychology professors: Mike McCarrey and Serge Piccinin. Mike and Serge took on the task of schooling me in the art of assertiveness training, and they did it with good humour, discipline and wisdom. Thanks, Mike and Serge, for steering me onto a path that I continue to explore decades later.

Table of Contents

About This Book

T his book has emerged from thirty years of therapeutic engagement with you, my clients, men and women struggling towards empowerment, often from a starting place of feeling overwhelmed and voiceless. Your resilience and ability to overcome has been truly inspirational. I have seen startling transformations, often manifested in the span of a few short weeks, revealing the capacity of the human spirit to thrive in spite of a history of deprivation, control and abuse.

I witnessed your transformations both in individual sessions and in the anxiety and assertiveness groups that I have facilitated over the years. The word *empowered* insisted its way into our dialogue, alerting me to deeper processes stirring below the surface like an unseen, but powerful underground stream. I became aware that something much more profound was unfolding in these sessions than simply managing anxiety or practicing a set of assertive skills.

I noticed that empowerment manifested in two ways: in developing mastery over your self – your emotions and mental states – and in having a voice in your relationships. Accordingly, I divided this book into two parts, each addressing these distinct aspects of empowerment. Part one focuses on self-empowerment while part two focuses on social-empowerment. Self-mastery becomes the foundation for social mastery. Tuning in to yourself, and respecting what you discover there, represents the genesis of all empowerment.

In self-empowerment you learn to master stress and anxiety by proactively shifting your emotions and mental states. Social-empowerment comes from freeing your assertive voice through practicing skills that help you to be more fully present in your relationships. An assertive way-of-being with others emerges from a set of values closely linked with the philosophy of empowerment: mutual respect, equality of rights, authenticity, ownership, responsibility, accountability and optimism in human relationships.

Empowerment requires making small acts of courage. It requires striving. It means taking a leap of faith in yourself, in spite of every instinct telling you to hide, to avoid and to be concerned with safety rather than growth. In making that act of faith, you find your voice.

Details of the case examples presented in this book have been altered in such a way as to disguise the identity and protect the anonymity of those involved. Some of the case examples are composites of more than one person.

Prologue

ANNE'S STORY

Anne grew up with well-defined values. Work hard at everything you do, her parents told her. Always finish what you start. Always do your best. Always be productive. It's important what others think of you. Don't argue with the teachers. Make sure you fit in. Don't draw attention to yourself. Do what you are told and don't rock the boat.

They made sure she had everything that she needed. They took her shopping and bought her the clothes that they thought would help her to fit in and belong.

Anne wanted very much to please others. She tried hard to figure out what other people wanted of her and gave her absolute best to live up to those expectations. She was a favorite with her teachers. "She's so easy to teach", they said, "not like some of the other kids". They wrote: "Anne plays well with others" in her report cards. It was true. She never fought with her schoolmates. Her parents felt pleased with her progress in school. They wanted her to be a teacher and that became her dream.

Eventually, she went to university where she continued to apply herself, never missing class and studying hard on evenings and weekends. She usually got straight A's and if she got anything less, she would become depressed, feeling like she was a failure. She would tell herself to try even harder next time. She felt stressed out by the demands of school and was relieved when she finally finished. School hadn't been much fun. She soon got a job as a teacher, but then she started to wonder if that was what she really wanted. Sometimes she would wake up in the middle of the night, her sleep disturbed by a pervasive feeling of emptiness. Something was missing but she didn't know what.

BETH'S STORY

From her earliest recollection, Beth's life was all about hiding. She would hide in a closet, under a bed, in a tree, under parked cars and trucks, or even behind the wheels of the freight trains that sat just outside her back yard.

Beth was born into a family that didn't want girls. Her parents doted on the boys while ignoring and neglecting even her most basic needs like clothes and health care. She was sent to play outdoors in nothing but her underwear, while her brothers were dressed in the latest styles. If she said she was sick, she was told to go to school anyway and stop complaining.

The oldest brother, four years her senior, delighted in his marked superiority in the family hierarchy. He learned that he could do whatever he wanted to Beth without any consequences. Anytime they were alone, he tormented her mercilessly. He would punch, pinch and bite her, or grab her by the hair shaking her until her neck ached. He would grab her hand and squeeze her knuckles till she screamed in pain. When she cried, he would claim innocence and feign any knowledge of the cause of his sister's distress. Her mother, unwilling to reprimand her beloved boy, would yell at Beth for crying. She would send the little girl to an upstairs room at the end of a hallway, separated from the rest of the family. First, though, she would give her something to cry about.

When she was eight, her brother found a new way to torment her. He would choke her until she passed out. When she reawakened, she discovered that she had wet herself while unconscious. Her mother became enraged, furious with her for this 'accident', and that meant even more punishment and isolation.

Things only got worse as she got older. In order to try to be safe, she would constantly be scanning everything and everyone. Always watch out, she learned. Never let your guard down. Be prepared for bad things to happen. Where was the next attack coming from? She never really felt safe, but it was easier when she was alone and isolated from others. It was best to be invisible.

WARREN'S STORY

Warren's father was an alcoholic. His father worked long hours and when he came home he needed a drink to relax and unwind. "Leave me alone, I've had a tough day at work'" he'd say to his young son when Warren tried to jump up on him as he walked through the door. "Let your father be, can't you see he's tired?" his mother would chime in. "Go outside and play."

Sometimes when his dad was at work, Warren would find his mother sitting on the couch in the dark, tears streaming down her cheeks. She wouldn't respond to him at all when he said: "Mom, mom. Are you OK? Are you going to make dinner? I'm hungry." Sometimes his mother packed a suitcase and then she would be gone for months. "She needs to see the doctors because she's sick," his dad would explain, but Warren didn't know what that meant or where his mother was going. Whenever he saw the suitcase by the door, he would be afraid that she wasn't coming back this time, but he didn't know how to say that or how to ask about what was happening. He was told to go play outside so he did. He was outside a lot. He climbed trees and explored abandoned buildings. He was on his own and so he learned to do things by himself. He watched other kids playing sports and he wanted to join in but he didn't know how. Anyway they would probably move again, like all the other times, so it seemed like a lot of work for nothing. I'm just an outsider, he thought.

"You are the gold."

PART ONE

Mastering Anxiety

1
The Nature of Empowerment

"This above all else: to thine own self be true."

Shakespeare

ELEMENTS OF EMPOWERMENT

Empowerment, like a diamond, has many facets. Elements of empowerment include: self-actualization, self-direction, having a voice, agency, intentionality, proactivity and equanimity.

EMPOWERMENT DEFINED

The word *power* originates from the 13th century, Anglo-French word *pouer,* which has the meaning: to be able. The idea of *ability,* fundamental to the original meaning of the word power, has been supplanted by the idea of having control over others. Other meanings of power are: strength, force, might and energy. Power as a verb means to effect movement through the application of force or energy as in: the motor powered the boat. Extending this idea to the psychological realm, the verb power also has the meaning of causing movement by inspiring others.

The prefix *em* in the word empowerment is derived from the word emic, which has the meaning: coming from the inside. Related words are: emanate and emit, indicating something coming from within and moving outwards. One definition of emanate is originate, to arise from within, while the meaning of emit is to give out. Combining the meanings of the prefix *em* with *power* results in the idea of empowerment as a realization of your inherent abilities that then impact on the world. Your latent talents arise within you and then flow outwards. Empowerment means that you have a voice, you express that voice and that your voice is heard.

SELF-ACTUALIZATION

In fiction, the notion of super-powers has been used as a literary device to explore the archetype of empowerment. The super-powers manifest as an energy or force having its origin in the person and emanating outwards. Heat vision is emitted to melt steel bars. The hero propels himself forward by leaping over tall buildings. An Amazonian woman of incredible power and strength casts her lasso of truth outwards into the world in her quest for justice and fairness.

Latent abilities become realized through the outward movement of energy, often to the super-hero's surprise and amazement. The archetypal message is that you are much more than you imagine yourself to be. These super-hero mythologies portray the psychological drive towards actualization and the fullest development of the psyche. They represent the urge to be all that you can be and to become all that you can become, to fully realize your potentials. As you develop and express your inner abilities, you become a presence in the world. That is self-actualization.

The movement of empowerment is like water bubbling up from an underground spring. This stream, sourced from the inner core of your being, flows out-wards, heralding the emergence of the fully developed personality. Individual abilities, skills and talents arise within you and then impact the outer world as those potentials become actualized.

This is the self-actualization nature of empowerment: to bring forth your abilities. The resulting expression of your true and authentic self can then inspire others, as the current of empowerment ripples outwards. Through self-actualization, you become empowered and make a contribution to the world. Your actualized self inspires and moves those whom you encounter.

Self-actualization means that you become all that you were meant to be; you become your fullest self. Think of a plant growing up from the earth. If that plant receives the essential conditions it needs to flourish – the right amount of sun, water and soil – it will self-actualize. It will become the fullest, most lush and beautiful plant it can possibly be. Of course, it cannot become an elephant. It can only be, more fully or less fully, what it truly is.

Self-actualization is about becoming fully and truly what you are by developing the skills and talents that are natural and meaningful to you. In doing so, you *become*.

> "If you bring forth what is within you, what you bring
> forth will save you."
>
> *Nag Hammadi Scrolls*

SELF-DIRECTION

Empowerment is about being guided by your self, first and fore-most. It means that you are resistant to the untoward influence of others. This requires proactivity and forethought, to develop a personal set of ethics and values that become the principles from which you act. Empowerment means that you find the courage to obey your self in the face of pressure to conform to some outer authority. You listen to your own inner voice, espe-cially when your internal voice conflicts with external demands.

Empowerment means that you identify your core values. These represent the rules that you will live by. There are cer-tain universal values that go hand and hand with the philos-ophy of empowerment. These include: authenticity; respon-sibility; accountability; universal human rights; and mutual equality and respect for all human beings. These empower-ment values are the foundation for assertive behaviour as a way of being-in-the-world and manifest in equal and mutu-ally respectful relationships.

The notion of having a set of rules that guide your behavior is as old as literature itself. One of the most ancient surviving writings in all of human literature is a Sumerian text entitled: Instructions of Šuruppak, dating back to 2900 BC. These instructions, written in Sumerian on clay tablets, take the form of admonitions from a father, King Šuruppak, to his son Ziasudra, who is the very first Noah figure depicted in stories of the Great Flood.

This ancient literature can be thought of as the first self-help book ever written, with suggestions given on how to live your life. King Šuruppak begins with:

"My son, let me give you instructions: you should com-ply with them!"

Many of his fatherly cautions take on a moral tone, pro-viding guidance on how to comport one's self. It presages the Ten Commandments with advice such as:

"You should not steal."

"You should not break into a house."

Much of the advice is singular, pertaining to specific situations:

"You should not pass judgment when you drink beer."

"You should not buy a donkey which brays."

One particular instruction is paraphrased multiple times in an apparent effort to underscore the importance of the message. These repeated bits of advice exhort the value of obedience to authority:

"You should submit to the respected."

"You should be humble before the powerful."

"Be obedient to your elder sisters and brothers as if they were your parents."

"The father is like a god: his words are reliable. The instructions of the father should be complied with."

There is no mention of what to do in case those in authority are making decisions that are not in your best interest. The notion of disagreement with authority is notable by its absence in this prescriptive list of rules to live by. Instead, this ancient narrative depicts Šuruppak, a King and a father, instructing others on how to live by extolling the virtues of obedience to those in power. The authority figure naturally espouses the values of compliance and submission to authority.

Of course, this advice is intended not solely for the king's son, but for the entire kingdom. These are rules to live by for everyone in the community, presented in the compelling narrative of a wise father advising his son. The message is that all should submit to those in power and comply with authority; that is how we will get along. This ancient story has been passed down over the millennia with unforeseen and disastrous consequences as unquestioning obedience to authority manifests in the loss of individual will, vulnerability to the influence of others and mass destructive behaviors justified by the explanation that 'I was just following orders.'

In a seventeenth-century parallel to that ancient Sumerian story, Shakespeare also tells the story of a father giving advice to his son. In Hamlet, Polonius gives parting counsel to his son Laertes, as he prepares to leave his home and go out on his own. Like Šuruppak, Polonius goes on at length with a list of instructions containing varying degrees of wisdom. A few familiar nuggets emerge from his exposition:

"Neither a borrower nor a lender be," and:

"Give every man thy ear, but few thy voice."

Shakespeare has Polonius concluding his admonitions with this unexpected wisdom:

"This above all else: to thine own self be true,

And it must follow, as the night the day,

Thou canst not then be false to any man."

Polonius takes a radically divergent viewpoint from that of King Šuruppak. He instructs his son that the most important thing – this, above all else – is to obey his inner sense of right and wrong, rather than yielding unquestioning obedience to those in authority. Polonius also wisely points out how living in a self-directed way will naturally result in authentic relationships with others. When you are true to yourself, you cannot be other than authentic with others.

To thine own self be true is a prescription for empowerment. When you are guided by your internal code, you live in an empowered and self-directed way. Your actions originate from you, rather than from compliance with external pressures. Empowerment means that you actualize your talents and abilities, and that your actions are guided by your inner sense of what is right and wrong.

HAVING A VOICE

Empowerment is about having a say in what happens to you. It's about having a voice and being a presence. You express yourself through your voice and articulate what you really think and feel.

If you study singing, a good voice teacher will help you to discover and release your own true and authentic voice. If you have been mimicking other singers, you will first need to overcome those habits in order to bring out your own, true, vocal instrument. Each person has their own unique voice based partly on the structure of their vocal cords, throat, head and chest. A good vocal coach can help you tune in to your own authentic voice and release it. Not everyone is blessed with a Stradivarius-quality vocal instrument, but there is something that resonates deeply with others when a vocalist sings from a place that is real and authentic. Conversely, the most challenging operatic passages ring hollow and evoke only boredom when the singer is not genuinely connected to the emotion of the song.

Empowerment is about finding your personal voice and expression as a human being. The truth and genuineness of your authentic voice inherently resonates with others in a powerful way. When you are empowered, you come out into the open and let others get to know you. You shine your light. Therefore, finding and expressing your voice results in increased intimacy and deepened connections with others.

AGENCY, INTENTIONALITY AND PROACTIVITY

Empowerment is about having the ability to make choices that profoundly affect your life's trajectory. When you are empowered, you become the agent of change in your life. Agency means that you decide how you live, not someone else. Empowerment means that you make the decisions in the things that will affect you. Agency is a key component of empowerment and is especially important for those in more powerless positions in society. As Gandhi said:

"The true measure of any society can be found in how it treats its most vulnerable members."

You can judge how much a society truly values empowerment by looking at how the most disempowered members of that society are treated. Does the society create the conditions under which the disempowered can move towards greater empowerment? Does the society make an effort to include the marginalized groups in the important decisions that may affect them? That would demonstrate a concern for their agency and thus for their empowerment.

Agency comes as a consequence of living from your *intention*. In developing empowerment, you formulate a clear intention and then convert it into an action; you carry out your plans and you act on your wishes. You live proactively rather than reactively and that requires an ongoing effort to tune in to yourself, in order to discover what it is that you truly want.

EQUANIMITY

Buddhists meditate partly in an effort to cultivate a state of consciousness described as equanimity. What exactly is equanimity? It involves a state of being associated with calmness, self-composure and non-reactivity in the face of stressful events. It is a state of inner poise that is not disturbed by worry, anxiety, pain or pleasure. Nor is it disturbed by external criticism, praise or negative life events. It represents composure in the face of provocation.

Equanimity can also be thought of as non-reactivity. Painful or difficult things do happen but when you are in a state of equanimity, you do not react to them. Instead, you maintain a state of composure and calmness. In Buddhism, human suffering is thought to arise from reacting to the events and emotions that you experience, rather than from the events themselves. As the Dalai Lama says:

"Pain is inevitable, but suffering is optional."

You can't entirely avoid stressful things; that's the pain that is an inevitable part of life. How much you suffer in reaction to those things, though, is up to you; that's the optional part.

Empowerment is closely related to equanimity in that empowerment is proactive and therefore non-reactive. You maintain self-direction even in the face of stressful events that challenge your composure. When you have equanimity, it is not easy for others to push your buttons, because your actions spring from a source within you. Equanimity and empowerment manifest in self-direction and in proactive living.

In self-empowerment, you maintain equanimity in the face of emerging emotions, even when powerful feelings such as anxiety and anger arise within you. When you have equanimity, you are not passively swept along by the current of those emotions. You don't lash out from anger or flee in fear. Instead, you regulate the intensity of your emotional states through practicing techniques such as breathing, coaching and altering what you are doing. These empowerment tools allow you to shift your state of consciousness and as a result you become free to act from your intention. Your emotions inform your actions rather than direct them.

In social-empowerment, you demonstrate equanimity in your relationships by maintaining a respectful attitude in your interactions. You take ownership for yourself while holding others accountable for their actions when necessary. You do that in a way that respects both yourself and the other person. Your interactions with others are self-determined rather than being in reaction to others. You maintain an attitude of mutual respect and equality of rights, regardless of what the other person does.

2
Mastering Stress

"Meditation is good, but sleep is better."

Dali Lama

STRESS AND THE CENTRAL NERVOUS SYSTEM

THE BASICS OF YOUR NERVOUS SYSTEM:
THE AUTONOMIC AND VOLUNTARY DIVISIONS

In order to understand stress management, it helps to first appreciate the nervous system. The central nervous system (CNS) is divided into the autonomic and the voluntary systems. The voluntary nervous system is under your conscious (voluntary) control. You decide to reach out for your cup of coffee and your hand happily obliges you and thus you get your morning caffeine fix. Thank you voluntary nervous system!

The autonomic (think automatic) nervous system operates, for the most part, outside of your conscious control. Your conscious mind is too busy making coffee to concern itself with body temperature, heart rate, blood flow and per-spiration. Your conscious mind would be overwhelmed trying to keep track of all those tasks, so those chores are instead left to your autonomic nervous system (ANS).

Imagine going down into a basement where you find numerous valves, dials and thermostats, all regulating var-ious systems in your house; that's what your ANS does for your body. You don't have to think about adjusting your heart rate and blood pressure as you walk up a flight of stairs because your ANS monitors the situation and takes care of it for you, all outside of your conscious awareness, like the regulating thermostats that stay out of sight in the basement.

THE SYMPATHETIC AND PARASYMPATHETIC BRANCHES

The types of chores controlled by your ANS can be divided into two categories: arousal chores and relaxation chores. One helps you *take care of business*, while the other helps you *take care of yourself.* These are governed by your sym-pathetic and parasympathetic nervous systems, respectively.

Your Sympathetic Nervous System

Your sympathetic nervous system (SNS) regulates arousal to deal with the various challenges that you face during the day. Your SNS can raise your heart rate; elevate your blood pres-sure; send blood flow to your limbs; focus your attention; and surge your glucose and adrenalin levels. It does all of this in the service of boosting your arousal to help you out when you feel challenged. It gives you alertness, focus and the phys-ical readiness to respond to the demands at hand.

However, not all challenges are equal. Threats and dan-gers represent more extreme levels of challenge. Your heart can pound in your chest, you may start to sweat profusely, and your attention might become so focused on the danger at hand that you start to have tunnel vision. Blood flows away from your internal organs and is re-routed to your limbs to help you fight or take flight. Adrenaline and glucose get pumped into your blood and provide a rapid, short-term boost to your energy level. If you don't take some physical action to burn up the adrenaline, you might start to tremble and shake. These symptoms will be all too familiar if you suffer from anxiety. Anxiety is a problem with your arousal system; it's is about having too much sympathetic nervous system activity. You've lost the balance between taking care of business and taking care of yourself.

Your Parasympathetic Nervous System

Your parasympathetic nervous system (PNS) manages relaxation tasks. It takes care of the four R's: relaxation, rest, restoration and rejuvenation. It's the part of your nervous system that is devoted to taking care of you. It's about healing and looking after yourself.

In parasympathetic activity, your heart rate and blood pressure decrease, breathing deepens and blood flows to your internal organs. You feel *safe* and your body starts to digest the food in your stomach. The agenda of your PNS is not to deal with challenge, but rather to restore, rejuvenate and repair. Your immune system begins to function when you are in a relaxed state. Your body tends to itself, repairing tissue damage.

A good night's sleep represents deep and profound PNS activity. During sleep, your mind transfers the events of the day from short-term memory to long-term memory. You need sleep to consolidate learning. Your mind and your body look after themselves and naturally heal and rejuvenate during sleep. The Dali Lama says:

"Meditation is good, but sleep is better!"

You can live without meditation but not without sleep.

Both the sympathetic and parasympathetic systems are essential for your well-being. Both are valuable and essential: sometimes you need to deal with challenge (taking care of business), and sometimes you need to rest (taking care of yourself). The two branches of your nervous system manage these very different functions in order to support you and keep you operating in a maximal way.

In society, there tends to be a greater value placed on sympathetic activities, which are regarded as active and productive. In contrast, parasympathetic activities are less valued and the importance and relevance of relaxation in mental health is not well understood. The core value espoused in the belief: "Always be productive" is a recipe for mental and physical health problems.

MASTERING STRESS THROUGH MAINTAINING BALANCE

Stress management is about maintaining a balance between your sympathetic and your parasympathetic nervous systems; this is the heart of stress management. What does a balance between these two very different parts of your nervous system look like?

Imagine going to work, being alert and focused, taking care of the various demands that you are confronted with over the course of the day. Then you go home, leave work at work, and take some time to relax. Maybe you go out to a show, play a sport or walk your dog. Maybe you spend time relaxing and bonding with your family. You get to bed early enough so that you get the full amount of sleep you need and as a result you wake up the next morning refreshed and ready to get back at it.

This represents a healthy balance between the sympathetic and the parasympathetic systems. In some parts of the day you are focused, alert and engaged. You take care of business and you accomplish things. You get things done.

In other parts of the day, you relax and you take care of yourself. You get into a deeply relaxed state where you feel peaceful and tranquil and your body heals itself. You have balance.

WHEN LIFE HAPPENS

But what if life doesn't cooperate with your balance? What if things were going very nicely, but all of a sudden there's more stress? Maybe a family member gets sick. Maybe there are extra deadlines and projects at work. Life happens and it's not always smooth sailing.

The reactive tendency is to stop doing the parasympathetic things to free up time to manage the extra demands. You don't go swimming because you need to work on the project with the looming deadline. You stop relaxing because you have to drive your relative to her medical appointments. The balance between the sympathetic and parasympathetic is lost and sympathetic activity becomes your chronic state as you live in a constant state of arousal. Worse, your sleep becomes affected. You wake up worrying and the restful quality of your sleep is lost. Those events should set off alarm bells that you are starting to become over stressed and that you need to do something differently to correct the situation, before it gets even more out of hand. That's the idea of proactivity; don't wait until you are completely stressed out, instead do something differently now, when you see the warning signs.

In practicing good stress management, you would need to actually increase the relaxation activities during stressful periods in your life. Parasympathetic activity becomes even more important when you are under stress. When the going gets tough, the tough relax. That's how you stay tough. Resilience is built through maintaining balance.

GETTING INTO A PARASYMPATHETIC STATE OF BEING

Charles Darwin suffered from chronic symptoms that we now would recognize as anxiety: heart racing; nervousness; sweating; trembling; anxiety around having guests; fear of being separated from his wife; and problems sleeping. In the 1850's, he was treated with hydrotherapy, also known as 'the water-cure.' This involved a few months stay in a spa where Darwin would take baths in water of varying temperatures, receive massage therapy and go for peaceful walks in nature. The spa was located some distance from his home, so he was also removed from the demands of his everyday life. This therapy helped Darwin immensely, although, after several months back at home and hard at work, his symptoms would once more return.

Hydrotherapy was effective because it increased parasympathetic activity. The spa baths, the massage and the walks in nature all served to put Darwin in a deeply relaxed, parasympathetic state. Furthermore, he was removed from the demands of his work and the related stress arising from his tendencies to work excessively. There was less need for activation of the sympathetic nervous system.

Massage therapy, yoga, acupuncture, meditation, cranial electrical stimulation, hypnosis and other forms of treatment involving relaxation continue to be effective treatments for anxiety in the present era. However, parasympathetic treatments, in themselves, may not be entirely sufficient in mastering anxiety.

Thought and behavioural patterns also need to be addressed or you can easily fall back into your old ways, in the same way that Darwin experienced his relapses. Patterns of excessive work without taking the time to relax need to be addressed in order to prevent a reoccurrence of anxiety in the future. The ideal treatment might involve a few months stay in a spa, combined with cognitive and behavioural change strategies. During your stay at the spa-retreat, you would practice skills such as breathing, coaching and doing (BCD) until they became second nature to you. You would learn to say no, to ask for what you want and you would practice setting limits with demands placed on you; these skills would then ensure that you maintain a balance as you return to your work and related challenges.

If you can't get to the spa for a few months, how do you get into a parasympathetic, deeply relaxed state? What kinds of things help you to achieve a state where your breathing becomes deep and slow, your heart rate decreases and you feel at peace? Remember, what works for someone else may not be right for you.

There are many activities that enhance relaxation. For example: yoga; meditation; hypnosis; relaxation training; connecting with your family; playing with your dog; going to the spa; and having a massage. You need to identify the specific activities that are effective for you. Then, build those things into your life so that they become a regular part of your routine. Be proactive. It helps if you appreciate that parasympathetic activities are as valuable and essential for your mental health as actively dealing with challenge. Play and relaxation balance work and striving.

CREATING A SPACE FOR YOURSELF

Physical environments can evoke relaxation. Do you have a physical space where you feel relaxed and at ease? If not, it is time to create one. It might be inside your home or outside in the backyard. If you do already have a space, take some time to evaluate it. Are there ways you might improve it so that it is even more conducive to your feelings of peacefulness and tranquility? Physical environments are powerful in shifting your state; the goal is to create a space that shifts you into a state of parasympathetic rest and relaxation.

Your space might be a room in your house. Maybe it's just one part of a room: a corner with a comfortable chair, good lighting, soothing colors, and some beautiful artwork on the wall. There might be a favourite book waiting for you on an end table while classical music is playing softly in the background. The space doesn't have to be big, but it does need to be inviting and appealing to your tastes. It is important that you decorate the space based on what you like. Take the time to tune in to yourself and determine what your tastes might be. Don't seek the opinions of others in your household. This is your individual space reserved for your tranquility.

What chair would be most comfortable for you? Do you prefer the sounds of the ocean, classical music, white noise or maybe just silence? What colors make you feel good? Are there works of art or specific objects that are particularly meaningful to you? Your tastes might change over time or you might just want something new to look at. Consider it to be a work in progress and make changes as you go along; adjust things that need adjusting. The bottom line is that when you enter this space, you naturally start to feel peaceful and comfortable and your body naturally starts to breathe deeply. That means that you are getting it right.

THE NURTURE OF NATURE

Darwin was impressed with the benefits of long peaceful walks in nature. Immersing yourself in the sensory world of nature induces parasympathetic activity and modulates your physiological arousal. Picture yourself walking on a beach: smell the sea, feel the warm white sand, listen for the sounds of the ocean and the distant cry of birds high over head. Even imagining that experience can lower your heart rate and deepen your breathing. Recall a walk in the forest with the sound of the wind in the trees, the butterflies fluttering by, the sound of your footsteps and the color of the leaves. Does your body change when you imagine that scene?

Your biology is profoundly connected with the natural world. The very cells and molecules of your being are from the earth and the sensory experience of nature regulates your biological systems. Your body is calmed and soothed by nature. Nature nurtures you.

USING MEDITATION TO GET INTO A PARASYMPATHETIC STATE OF BEING

There are many forms of meditation, but all tend to shift your state towards parasympathetic activity. When you meditate, your mind starts to quiet and your body relaxes and releases tension. Your breathing deepens. A quiet mind and a relaxed body stimulate rejuvenation and healing and help you maintain a healthy balance between the parasympathetic and the sympathetic. Once you have mastered the art of meditation, you can use it anywhere at anytime; there is no equipment necessary.

STAYING MEDITATION AND QUIET MIND

One form of meditation is called *staying* meditation. Staying meditation, like Samādhi (Brown, 2006), involves training attention to persist in a singular focus. You place your attention on some object and you have it stay there. It's as if your attention is a flashlight and you are going to shine that light on a particular place and keep it there.

Buddhists refer to the anxious mind as monkey-mind because it is always active, chattering and jumping from one thing to the next. Getting your anxious monkey-mind to stay calmly focused may not be easy at first, but it can be learned with practice. A natural by-product of the staying is that you start to develop *quiet mind*. That means you experience a moment where there are no thoughts and no images in your mind at all. Maybe you are aware of your body resting comfortably in the chair, but there are no mental distractions, there is just pure awareness; that's quiet mind. At first you may have only a second or two of quiet mind, but as you practice staying, the duration of quiet mind increases.

INSTRUCTIONS FOR STAYING MEDITATION

The following instructions outline helpful steps in developing a staying mind. As you learn to sustain attention, your mind will naturally tend to become quieter and more peaceful.

Staying and Returning

Start by making yourself comfortable. Take a deep breath and breathe out slowly, letting your eyes close with the exhalation of breath. Guide your attention to your feet. Become aware of the sensations that are there. You may notice the soles of your feet against your shoes. Maybe you notice your heels or the balls of your feet. Perhaps your attention goes to a warmth or coolness in your feet or a tingling in the toes. Keep your attention in your feet until you become aware of the sensation that stands out the most for you. It might be in both feet or more in one foot than the other. Become aware of the sensation that is the most vivid for you.

Once you have found that sensation, it becomes the focus for your staying practice. Keep your attention focused on that sensation. If your attention wanders and you lose the capture of the sensation, as soon as you notice that happening, gently but firmly bring your attention back. You may have to do that more than once.

Go ahead and do that for one minute. (If someone is helping you by reading these instructions, they can keep time for you and let you know when the minute is up. Otherwise you can set a timer before you begin.)

Counting the Breaths

The next step involves counting your breaths while you keep your attention staying in your feet. You will count breaths starting with ten and working downwards towards one.

With your attention in your feet, take a deep breath and slowly breathe out. At the end of the exhalation of breath, think "ten" and think it into your feet. As you have the thought "ten" imagine it is right in your feet, exactly where your attention is focused. This helps with your staying. At the end of the next breath, do the same with "nine." The goal is to go from "ten" all the way down to "one" while you maintain the staying throughout. If you lose the capture of your feet at some point, start over at "ten." Notice at what point you lost the staying. If you made it to eight, then that is your personal best. Now you will try to beat that personal best by going all the way down to seven and then beyond. One thing that can help is intensification.

Intensification

Imagine that your attention is a flashlight and you are shining that light on your feet. You want to keep it focused on your feet without wavering. Think of your flashlight as having a dial that allows you to intensify the beam. You can adjust the intensity of your attention by making it stronger or by backing it off.

Guide your attention back to your feet as you have been doing in steps one and two. Focus in on the sensation that stands out the most for you. Now, intensify your focus; zoom your attention in so that you become hyper-aware of the sensation. When you feel your attention intensify, gently back it off to its previous level of attention. Notice that you can intensify your focus and you can also back it off.

If your personal best was "eight', as you approach "eight", intensify your focus. Zoom your attention in to your feet. Keep that level of intensification up until you get to "seven." Congratulations, you've just achieved a new personal best! Now you can back off the intensity and continue on your way to "six" and "five" with a more relaxed staying mind.

Once you can repeatedly go from ten to one without losing your focus, you no longer need to count the breaths. It's a transitory strategy to help you expand the duration of your staying mind and thus increase the experience of quiet mind. You can practice staying mind everyday, even if it's only for a few minutes. Practice for short intervals, but do so repeatedly. Focus on improving your skill as you practice.

Evoking a state of consciousness where your mind is quiet and focused means that you stimulate parasympathetic activity. That helps to restore the balance in your nervous system. It reduces anxiety, builds resilience and improves attention. It means that you are mastering stress by being proactive. You are not waiting for the stress to happen and then reacting to it; you're taking action ahead of time. Proactivity is a key element of empowerment.

ACTIVITIES THAT EVOKE PARASYMPATHETIC RELAXATION

In order to maintain a balance between the parasympathetic and sympathetic systems, it is important to get into a deeply relaxed state everyday. What are the things that make you feel calm, peaceful and relaxed? What do you do so that your body begins to breathe deeply, your muscles relax and your mind becomes quiet and peaceful? Here is a list of some activities that are associated with parasympathetic activity. It is important to make your own list because what works for one person may not be effective for someone else.

AVENUES TO A PARASYMPATHETIC STATE OF MIND

- Massage therapy
- Yoga
- Diaphragmatic Breathing
- Hot tub
- Relaxation
- Connecting with family
- Being held
- Playing with pets
- Being in nature
- Reading
- Prayer
- Going to church or some other sacred place
- Meditation
- Hypnosis
- After intense exercise
- Listening to music
- Playing music
- Creating art

3

An Empowered State of Consciousness

"I felt like: Well, just bring it on."

Woman describing her newly discovered
empowered state of consciousness.

What exactly are states of consciousness? States have been defined as unique patterns of brain activation that occur at some particular point in time (Siegal, 1999). In the same way that neurons are the fundamental units of the brain, states are the fundamental units of the mind. States of consciousness are reflected in the distinctive way that your brain lights up under different conditions and in response to various situations. Those brain activations can be accompanied with related emotions, memories, attentional processes, cognitions, behaviors, perceptions, physiology and even an altered sense of self.

States can be linked to intense emotions: an angry state, a depressed state or a euphoric state. Think about what you experience when you are very angry. Recall the last few times you felt angry. What happened in your body, in your thoughts, in how you responded to others? What was your physical posture associated with being angry? That's your angry state.

The state of equanimity is associated with calmness, compassion, inner peace and unconditional regard for yourself and others. You are less reactive in this state. When your brain lights up in a pattern associated with equanimity, your breathing becomes deeper, your heart rate slows and you feel peaceful. The emotions associated with the state of equanimity are very different from the state associated with anxiety and anger.

There has been much discussion in the psychology literature about affect regulation – in other words emotion regulation – but very little has been said about state regulation. We lose an important set of modulation skills as a result of overlooking states of consciousness. Learning how to shift your state is a fundamental skill in mastering anxiety and in developing empowerment.

SYMPATHETIC AND PARASYMPATHETIC STATES OF CONSCIOUSNESS

Two common states of consciousness are associated with activity in either the sympathetic or the parasympathetic parts of your central nervous system, introduced in the preceding chapter. These states of mind can be thought of as arousal states (sympathetic) or relaxed states (parasympathetic). These states of mind are uniquely distinct from each other and you may therefore have a different sense of yourself – your identity – when you are in these different states.

SYMPATHETIC & PARASYMPATHETIC FUNCTIONS

SYMPATHETIC AROUSAL: TAKING CARE OF BUSINESS

↑	10	Life Threat / Threat/ Danger	Perceptual changes: Tunnel vision, time slows down, deafness, out of body, unreality
↑	8	Panic Attack	Fight/flight
↑	6	Sky Diving / Roller Coaster	Surge of adrenalin, glucose, cortisol
↑	4	Job Interview / Taking a Test at School / Work Tasks	Increased heart rate, blood pressure Sweating, flushed face, muscle tension Rapid, shallow breathing, on edge
↑	2	Challenge, External Focus	Blood flows to limbs, away from internal organs, butterfly's, nausea, queasy

ALTERED STATE

NORMAL WAKING STATE

Eyes open, relaxed attention, alert but not vigilant

PARASYMPATHETIC RELAXATION: TAKING CARE OF YOURSELF

↓	2	Safety, Internal Focus Sound/ Smells of Nature	Rest, Relaxation, Restoration, Rejuvenation
↓	4	Touch, Holding a Baby	Decreased heart rate, blood pressure Blood flows to internal organs, digestion
↓	6	Yoga, Hypnosis, Meditation	Diaphragmatic breathing
↓	8	Relaxation, Hot Tub Massage	Relaxed body, Quiet mind Parasympathetic Healing
↓	10	Deep Sleep	Short term into long-term memory Body heals, immune system functions

ALTERED STATE

Consciousness and Sympathetic Arousal

Your normal waking state involves moderate alertness and physiological arousal. Your attention is focused, but not so much so that you can't easily shift to something else that might catch your attention. This represents a low level of sympathetic arousal.

In response to challenges such as work tasks, your level of arousal increases; you become more alert and attention becomes more focused on the job at hand. There is an increase in muscular tension as your body also prepares to respond to the demand.

At higher levels of arousal, attention becomes increasingly focused and directed to signs of threat or danger. Your attentional field narrows and non-threat information is ignored. At extreme levels of arousal, your perception can shift into tunnel vision. Your perception becomes absorbed entirely with the danger while any peripheral information is blocked out.

At the body level, arousal states are associated with activation of the sympathetic nervous system. Intense emotions of fear and anxiety emerge as you prepare for fight or flight. Your body experiences a physiological arousal in readiness for physical activity; your heart beats fast, your muscles tighten and your mind becomes alert and vigilant to signs of danger and threat. Your chemistry changes dramatically in preparation for the fight/flight response.

Awareness in this state is experienced in a very different way from when you are in a relaxed state. In a heightened arousal state, other parts of your brain become activated that are not usually front and center in your daily life. You are now operating from a substantially different brain from the one that usually guides your actions. You are in an altered state of consciousness, one involving highly focused attention accompanied with intense arousal, hyper-vigilance and alertness. This state is associated with beta wave patterns in your brain.

Consciousness and Parasympathetic Relaxation

The parasympathetic state of consciousness manifests most profoundly when you are in a relaxed and peaceful sleep. On the physical level, your breathing becomes deeper and slower and is centralized in the diaphragm. Your body releases tension and your attention drifts and flows as your brain dreams. At lesser levels of parasympathetic activity, you are awake but relaxed and mostly focused inwards. The relaxation response and meditative states would fall into that level of parasympathetic activity. Daydreaming would also be parasympathetic but less deep than sleep or meditation.

During parasympathetic activity, the goals are the four R"s: rest, relaxation, restoration and rejuvenation. Your body delegates energy to healing and restoring itself. Your immune system starts to function more fully to help with any healing that needs to take place. Your mind dreams as the experiences of the day are assimilated and stored in long-term memory. Your body repairs itself.

When you are in a parasympathetic state of consciousness, your mind drifts easily from one thing to another. It may become completely quiet and at rest, similar to what happens during meditation. You feel calm and at peace with yourself. There are distinct brain wave patterns associated with a relaxed, meditative state of consciousness, known as alpha waves. Increased parasympathetic activity, evident in deep sleep, is associated with delta waves.

Shifting Gears, Shifting States

You naturally switch back and forth between different states during the course of the day. You switch states effortlessly and often without being aware of it, like an automatic car shifts gears in response to environmental conditions. You enter your place of work and you become more alert in order to focus your attention on the tasks at hand. Your heart rate and blood pressure increase slightly in preparation for the work to be done. There are subtle changes in your blood chemistry as glucose and small amounts of adrenalin are released in the service of enhanced arousal. At the end of your workday, you go home and put your feet up and your heart rate drops, your breathing slows and your blood flow shifts to your internal organs. All of this state shifting occurs with little or no conscious thought. Outside of your awareness, though, your brain assesses the situation at hand and shifts you into the most helpful state for that particular situation.

THE STATE OF FLOW IN PEAK PERFORMANCE

Empowerment is a state of consciousness similar to a state of *flow* that has been associated with peak performances in sports and performing arts (Csikszentmihalyi, 1990). Flow is a state of mind in which you are completely immersed in your experience. Your mind is free from conflicts and distractions because you are completely absorbed in what you are doing. Your performance becomes optimal when you are in that state, and you may even surpass your previous personal best. You surprise yourself, like the super-hero discovering unexpected abilities within herself.

The state of flow can occur naturally throughout the day. Csikszentmihalyi, in his 1997 book: *Finding Flow, The Psychology of Engagement with Everyday Life*, details how flow can be found in everyday life experiences:

"This complete immersion in the activity may occur in a social situation, as when good friends talk with each other, or when a mother plays with her baby. What is common to such moments is that consciousness is full of experiences, and these experiences are in harmony with each other. Contrary to what happens all too often in everyday life, in moments such as these what we feel, what we wish, and what we think are in harmony. These exceptional moments are what I have called flow experiences."

So when you are in that state of consciousness, your experience *flows* in a natural and uninhibited way. Flow involves a deep state of immersion, concentration and absorption in the activity that you are engaged with, so much so that other things can fade from awareness (Csikszentmihalyi, 1990). In flow, your performance not only peaks but it is also experienced as spontaneous and effortless. Internally, you feel a sense of harmony; everything comes together and works toward the same goal.

Sports psychologists train elite athletes to proactively access a state of flow in order to attain peak performance. The pertinent skills for shifting states of consciousness are derived primarily from the field of hypnosis. Hypnotic techniques have been used for hundreds of years in accessing and altering various states of consciousness. These skills can be learned by anyone, not just elite athletes.

The skill of shifting your state of consciousness will help you in mastering anxiety and in developing greater influence over your mental states. Accessing a state of flow and other empowered states of consciousness, frees you from anxiety. If you are in a state of equanimity, you have no anxiety. If you are in a state of flow, your actions become spontaneous and effortless and you are without self-consciousness. You have internal harmony. The first step in learning these important life skills is to be able to identify the desired state of consciousness.

YOUR EMPOWERED STATE OF CONSCIOUSNESS

Becoming familiar with your empowered state of consciousness is the first step in eventually being able to shift into it when you chose to. You become familiar with your empowerment state by identifying accompanying bodily sensations, physical posture, emotions, words and imagery.

DESCRIPTIONS OF AN EMPOWERED STATE OF CONSCIOUSNESS

Here are some descriptions of empowered states of consciousness:

"I think of the phrase: I'm on solid ground. I even feel more grounded."

"I feel lighter. It's mainly in my shoulders. They're more straight."

'I am more upright. I actually feel taller. There's a warmth in my chest."

"I feel strong."

"I feel calm."

"I have the image of superwoman!"

"It's an attitude, like: 'Well just bring it on.' I feel like, whatever it is, I can handle it."

"I look people in the eye."

"I picture myself as much bigger."

"I feel calm and proud of myself. I'm really pumped. It's the same sort of feeling just after I'm finished working out at the gym, where I feel relaxed and I feel good about myself."

"I see a big, strong oak tree."

"It feels like a huge weight is lifted off my shoulder. Then I have this certainty that I can do it again."

"My jaw is more relaxed. That clenching is gone. I feel hot. I feel a rush, like an adrenalin rush and I'm thinking: I know I have value."

Notice that the descriptions of empowerment include physical sensations and postures (more upright, shoulders straighter, relaxed jaw, lightness), images (superwoman, a taller self, a big oak), emotions (relaxed, strong, calm, proud, grounded, confident) and specific words or sayings (bring it on, I know I have value, I'm on solid ground).

HYPNOTIC ANCHORS

These physical sensations, images, feelings and words can be used as cues that will help you to shift into the accompanying state whenever you chose to access it. In hypnosis, these cues are referred to as *anchors*, as they anchor you into the state. Over time, the anchors become increasingly wired together with the state of consciousness. The more you shift into that state, the more the anchors become paired with the state through a process called classical conditioning.

Learning to evoke these anchors results in being able to pro-actively shift your state of consciousness. You deliberately bring up the cues and doing so shifts you into an empowerment state of consciousness. With repeated practice, these state shifts can occur very rapidly. The next chapter describes in more detail a number of methods designed to help you shift your state of consciousness.

4

Transitions in States of Consciousness

"We've done dental hygiene, but not mental hygiene.
We know how to prevent cavities,
but we don't teach children how to be resilient,
how to cope with stress on a daily basis"

Sat Bir Khalsa

METHODS FOR SHIFTING STATES OF CONSCIOUSNESS

As a parent, you act instinctively to shift your children's states of consciousness. You get your children ready for bedtime by giving them a bath, putting on pyjamas and reading them a bedtime story. As these activities unfold, your child shifts from an aroused (sympathetic) state to a relaxed (parasympathetic) state. If all goes well, your child falls into a deep and restful sleep as you read them the bedtime story. Many parents do this intuitively, without awareness that they have been involved in the shifting of states of consciousness. It has not been part of our educational curriculum to provide instruction on how to shift states, in spite of the commonness and significance of those skills.

How important are state shifts? Attempts at altering states of consciousness are interwoven with the history of humanity. The earliest graphic representations of ancient man portray shamans using rituals to alter their consciousness. In the present day, loud drums, repetitive music and drugs are commonly used for the same purpose. Much of the economy is based on the promotion of products and activities designed to shift your state of consciousness. The promise is that if you use their product you will feel more confident or have some other positive state shift. Those dubious claims can be effective marketing strategies because they are based on the human motivation to shift your state of consciousness.

There are many methods for altering your states including hypnosis, prayer, meditation, drugs, sexual activity, dancing, intense physical activity and deprivation through fasting or limiting sensory input. However, there are also simpler and less drastic ways to accomplish the same goal.

USING YOUR BREATH TO SHIFT YOUR STATE

Regaining control over your body is a crucial part of self-empowerment and in mastering anxiety. How you breathe plays a key role in determining the amount of anxiety that you experience at any time. Rapid and shallow breathing increases your anxiety dramatically while deep breathing diminishes it. Although there are many ways to breathe deeply, there is one form of deep breathing in particular that is extremely beneficial, known as diaphragmatic breathing.

If you observe a child or a pet sleeping, you will notice that their breathing comes primarily from the belly. The abdomen moves gently in and out while the upper body makes only the slightest movement. Observe a new born infant and you will see an example of perfect diaphragmatic breathing, accomplished without instructions of any kind!

What exactly is diaphragmatic breathing? The diaphragm is a dome-shaped muscle that horizontally dissects your body and separates your lungs from your intestines. In diaphragmatic breathing, the inhalation of breath is accompanied by a flattening of the dome shape that results in your belly pushing outwards. Exhaling restores the dome shape and results in your belly pulling in. The motion naturally occurs around your entire core but is most noticeable in the belly. When you breathe diaphragmatically your upper chest and shoulders remain relaxed and motionless.

Diaphragmatic breathing shifts your state from sympathetic to parasympathetic, thereby reducing your anxiety. This deep and full breathing is a naturally occurring function of the body that, for many people, has been lost over the years. Diaphragmatic breathing is the peak performance of breathing and bolsters the body's ability to both heal itself and to maximize performance. You can breathe diaphragmatically in any situation, whether you are meditating or running a marathon.

Instructions For Diaphragmatic Breathing

Place one hand above your belly button and the other hand higher up on your chest. As you slowly breathe in, the air will come in and move down towards the bottom of your lungs. Your belly will inflate and your belly hand will move outwards as you breathe in. Your chest hand will be still and have no movement at all. You will need to use your abdominal muscles to help out, like a belly dancer. Push your belly out as you breathe in. You are mastering diaphragmatic breathing when your belly hand is pushed out as you inhale and pulled in as you exhale. Your chest hand remains still, as all of your breathing becomes focused in your belly. Your neck and shoulders will feel relaxed. If you find this difficult, master the abdominal in-and-out activity first, then develop a relaxed and motionless chest.

Practice this breathing six times a day for six breaths. Do this for two weeks and you will be surprised to discover that your body will start to breathe diaphragmatically on its own, as this becomes your natural way of breathing.

How to Practice: Brief, Repeated and Perfect

All learning takes place through repetition and practice. The best practice takes the form of *brief, repeated* and *perfect* forms of the desired behavior or skill. For example, if you were practicing a difficult piece on the piano, a good way to practice would be to briefly play the passage, slowed down and fingered as perfectly as possible. It is better not to practice for hours on end, due to fatigue, boredom and behavioral drift away from the more perfect articulation of the piece. It is counter-productive to practice sloppy playing as now you not only have to learn the correct phrasing, but you also must unlearn the incorrect playing.

Repetition is essential for learning and so practicing the piece several times a day for a few weeks would reap enormous improvement in the performance. A few minutes of practice several times a day over the course of a few weeks is not very onerous or time demanding and allows for more sustained attention, which in turn maximizes the learning.

How does this apply to diaphragmatic breathing?

Practice briefly might mean taking six diaphragmatic breaths, but you would do this several times a day; that's the repeated part. Taking six breaths will take about a minute and so six times a day would amount to only six minutes of practice. Do this every day for two weeks. It's not a big time commitment, but it is a commitment in persistence over time. In order to change anything, you have to repeatedly do something differently than what you have been doing. You will be surprised to see how fast you can learn new skills when using these simple principles.

What about the perfect part? Isn't perfectionism actually a part of anxiety? Yes it is – especially when it's applied to everything you do and when perfectionism is applied retrospectively. In other words, looking back at what you just did to find fault, only keeps your anxiety going. It's not helpful in improving your performance. On the other hand, it is helpful to apply the idea of perfection prospectively, before the task. What would the perfect performance look like? Imagining yourself accomplishing the task perfectly gives you an exemplar or ideal of what you are trying to attain. Then you can use that model to inform your practice. It's where you set the bar that you are trying to move towards.

As previously described, in diaphragmatic breathing only the belly moves, while the shoulders, neck and upper chest remain still and comfortably relaxed. That's what perfect diaphragmatic breathing looks like and that's the goal that you are working towards. If your chest is moving along with your belly, stop. Modify your practice to improve it. Don't persist in practicing bad stuff because it's counter-productive. Practicing bad habits sets you back because you will have to unlearn what you just practiced. You don't start with perfection, but you do need to be moving your performance towards perfection as you practice.

Practicing for short intervals allows you to focus more fully on what you are doing without being distracted. Over time, your mind naturally tends to wander. You are more able to concentrate fully on the skill that you are trying to master when you keep your practice times short. Furthermore, when you give your full attention to your practice, you are more able to detect small imperfections that you can then modify. You get a little better with each practice. That means you're getting it right!

USING POSTURES TO SHIFT YOUR STATE

Another powerful tool for using your body to shift your state of mind is through the use of body postures. What is not well known, outside of yoga devotees, is that different physical postures can be used to induce various mental and emotional states. Dr. Felicitas Goodman, an innovative anthropologist and linguist, devoted much of her career to studying and exploring ritual body postures found in prehistoric cave paintings and other early art, some dating back 40,000 years. She identified over sixty postures and her discoveries were detailed in her books: When the Spirits Ride the Wind; and, Ecstatic Trance.

Each of the postures is associated with a specific type of experience. These postures were used, in conjunction with persistent rhythmic stimulation such as drumming, to facilitate the experience of shamanic journeying. Journeys were undertaken for various purposes, one of which was healing. In fact, shamans acted as the first doctors, psychotherapists and priests, long preceding the later emergence of those disciplines. Unfortunately, much of shamanic knowledge and wisdom has been lost over time as the new fields of medicine and psychology supplanted this ancient wisdom.

The Healing Posture

Postures are not only used for shamanic purposes, but they can also be helpful in enhancing peak performance in the modern day world. One of these postures, known as the Healing posture (also known as the Bear posture), is particularly beneficial and can be easily adapted to everyday use as an empowerment tool for shifting your state of mind.

In my work with traumatized individuals, I frequently observe clients becoming emotionally overwhelmed and distressed, as traumatic experiences from the past intrude into the present moment. Assuming this posture helps to alleviate that distress. Similar to the effects of diaphragmatic breathing, the posture can bring about a fairly rapid recovery from episodes of sympathetic over-arousal and induce a state of parasympathetic healing. It helps you to regain a sense of control over your body and your mental states. Like diaphragmatic breathing, it can be easily learned in a few moments. It becomes another tool that is readily accessible to you, wherever you might happen to be.

The posture can enrich and augment the effects of other therapies. It can easily be used in conjunction with other therapeutic modalities such as hypnosis, relaxation, meditation, cognitive therapy and EMDR. Simply assuming the healing posture seems to enhance the effectiveness of any of those therapies.

The healing posture shifts your state of mind into greater mental clarity, alertness and reduced fatigue. Fortuitously, this posture often spontaneously results in diaphragmatic breathing. Combining diaphragmatic breathing with the healing posture not only has a powerful impact on your state of consciousness, but also strengthens a sense of mastery and control over your body.

The original posture is done standing up, with eyes closed and mouth slightly open. Making some slight modifications in the posture allows you to readily assume it in any situation and to be able to comfortably maintain it over a long period of time.

Instructions For the Healing Posture

In order to assume the healing posture from a sitting position, begin by having your feet flat on the ground and parallel, about six inches apart. Rest your elbows gently against your sides, then cross your hands across your abdomen, just above the belly button. One hand should be held gently in the other. Go with how your hands naturally fall across your abdomen as you keep your elbows touching against your sides. Your head is slightly tilted back and your chin is slightly elevated.

Notice any changes in how you feel, both mentally and emotionally. Also notice what happens to your breathing when
you assume this healing posture.

The posture is surprisingly easy to assume and comfortable to maintain. It can be learned in just a few moments and
thus easily added to your repertoire of empowerment tools.
It integrates naturally with diaphragmatic breathing, reduces
distress and helps your body to recover from stress.

The Posture of Empowerment

Your body naturally assumes a posture that accompanies
the feeling of empowerment. Your physical being becomes
in harmony with your emotional experience. Whenever you
experience a moment of empowerment, take a few minutes
to become familiar with the posture associated with that
experience. Later, you will deliberately assume this posture
in order to shift your state into one of empowerment.

For many people the posture of empowerment has a
theme of ascension: the head is slightly elevated, the shoulders
are back and the chest moves out and up. You stand taller.
This physical posture is associated with opening up rather
than closing down. It also is associated with a sense of being
grounded and feeling solid on your feet. However, these are
general tendencies and what is most important is that you
become familiar with your unique posture of empowerment.

USING IMAGERY TO SHIFT YOUR STATE

An important peak performance skill in sports psychology is
the use of mental imagery. In preparation for their performance,
elite athletes are trained to first visualize themselves succeeding
in the activity in which they are about to engage. Not only do

they see themselves succeed, but they also picture this success unfolding in an easy and effortless way, from the start to the finish of the performance. It's the ideal performance; it's fluid and masterful. It's the peak in peak performance.

Imagery is used to visually set the bar for the performance to which you aspire. Then, the body follows the directions of the mind. Imagining success is an important tool in mastering anxiety and in allowing your natural skills and talents to emerge.

Imagining Success

Self-empowerment results from having control over your mental processes and from appreciating the association between your mind, behavior and body. Many people are unaware of the connection between mental imagery, emotional states and subsequent performance. If imagery skills were taught early on in life, they would become second nature as tools for goal achievement. These tools promote resilience and enhance self-actualization.

Imagining success acts in a positive, self-fulfilling way as it shifts your state into one associated with excellence and ease. Imagery promotes peak performance in any activity in which you might engage. It is also a easily learned technique that can be readily taught to most people, including young children. These skills are particularly important for children, as they naturally tend to have greater imagery capability than adults. As you grow beyond your teen years, your imagery vividness tends to diminish, as you become increasingly focused on the external world. However, even if you have a poor capacity for imagery, it is possible, through practice, to increase the vividness of your imagery.

If children were taught to practice peak performance visualizations, it is likely that their imagery capacity would be sustained into adulthood. Imagery ability would be reinforced through enhanced performance and would therefore be strengthened over time. Adult consciousness would be transformed and enhanced imagery capability would become the standard mental phenomenon of the mature brain.

But how does imagining success apply to non-athletes? Can those skills be used in activities other than sports? Peak performance has been typically restricted to a small group of very high performing athletes. What about the rest of us?

The good news is that these skills can be used in everyday life to help you accomplish any goal that you have. More importantly, peak performance skills are fundamental to good mental health. These skills promote well-being, enhance quality of life and inhibit anxiety, depression and emotional distress.

You can go through life visualizing success in any activity: simply see yourself succeeding in whatever is going to happen next. For example, if you are going out to dinner with your spouse, take a moment to visualize that experience going incredibly well. It will be the peak performance of having dinner with your spouse – whatever that means to you. If you have never taken the time to define what that does mean, these visualizations will become a source of surprise and discovery. It's a way of tuning in to yourself and uncovering what it is that you would truly like. Repeatedly visualizing yourself succeeding in the routine matters of daily living transforms the way you experience life. It solidifies core feelings of intentionality and self-direction as you cultivate a habit of proactivity.

Remembering Success

The skill of visualizing success can be applied to both the past and the future. Recalling success means that you bring up memories of successful experiences while imagining success involves predicting success in the future.

In sports psychology, athletes are encouraged to pay particular attention to any outstanding performance. For example, a golfer who makes the perfect swing learns to take a moment to retrieve that memory, as vividly as possible, using kinaesthetic and visual imagery: What did that swing feel like? How did I experience it in my body? How did my hands feel on the club? How far apart were my feet? Was there a sound associated with it? A phrase?

Identifying those cues help to make the past experience more accessible to you in future challenges. Bringing up the memory of success, in a vivid way, allows you to access that state and skill performance again and again. You not only practice the skill, but you also practice accessing the memory of the peak performance of that skill.

The three aspects of skill learning – brief, repeated and perfect – can be applied to the mental rehearsal of recalling peak moments. Past success, whether recent or remote, can be brought into conscious awareness repeatedly (several times a day), briefly (for a few seconds) and perfectly (specific memories of the most successful experiences). The repetition helps you to build a pathway in your brain that you can then traverse in order to access a similar state of peak performance in the future.

Words Associated With the Empowerment State

A sprinter might think: "I'm taking care of business," whenever she vividly recalls the details of a past peak performance in sprinting. The association between the thought and her state of mind is strengthened through repetition. The verbal cue becomes associated with the recall of the memory, like a handle on a suitcase. The thought allows her to grab the experience from her memory bank and pull it fully into consciousness. The hypnotic anchor acts as an empowerment tool that enables her to shift her state of consciousness in preparation for the task at hand. But why stop there? Why not use multiple anchors to help shift your state?

LEARNING FROM HYPNOSIS: USING MULTIPLE ANCHORS TO SHIFT YOUR STATE

In the field of hypnosis, it is known that combining a set of cues – involving a variety of sensory experiences – will act as a powerful tool in shifting states of consciousness. The mnemonic PIES (Posture, Image, Emotion and Saying) will help you to recall a set of anchors associated with your unique empowerment state of consciousness.

Posture – Image – Emotion – Saying (PIES)

Evoking PIES can shift your state rapidly into an empowerment state of consciousness. Your homework was to identify those anchors. You have taken the time to become familiar with the physical posture associated with that state of consciousness, perhaps it is: shoulders back, arms relaxed and knees slightly bent. You noticed a physical sensation of lightness in your chest. You bring up your PIES image: you see yourself as a giant, ten feet tall, powerful. You recall the emotion that you felt when previously in that state: a feeling of being confident. The saying that you have identified is: "Well, just bring it on".

In this example, using PIES means that you proactively assume an upright posture, see yourself as a giant, have a feeling of confidence and think the words: "Well, just bring it on." In doing those four things – it takes a matter of seconds – you shift into an empowered state of consciousness. Now, you are ready for what happens next. Bring it on.

Contrast that with the anxiety-state inducing habits of hunching your shoulders, shifting your gaze downwards, visualizing things going catastrophically wrong, feeling the emotion of fear and telling yourself:

"I can't do this; I should get out of here!"

How you enter the situation is critical in determining the final outcome. Depending on which state you evoke, the trajectory you set in motion will end up in radically different places. You shape that trajectory through your use of PIES; it means that proactivity rules the day.

EMPOWERMENT THROUGH MEANING AND PURPOSE

When you live in a way that is meaningful to you, it feels that your life has purpose and direction. It is like living in in a spiritual state of consciousness. That spiritual state allows you to encounter stress with greater equanimity.

The right path is a method that I developed in the 1970's as a response to events in my life. Using the right path technique resulted in my present career in psychology. In spite of my own positive results in utilizing this method, I found it hard to believe that the outcomes were not merely co-incidental. Eventually, I overcame enough of my initial skepticism to use the technique with others who were at a point where they needed to make significant changes in their lives. As a result, I was privileged to witness transformations in individuals who had been, up to that point, very stuck in their lives, feeling incapacitated and not knowing what to do next.

The right path is derived from that common bit of folk wisdom that we are all here for a reason; everyone has a purpose. There is a reason you are here, something you are supposed to be doing, certain people that you are meant to be with and specific places you are meant to be. That is the right path. Everyone has one.

From a spiritual perspective, you are on your right path when you are making the contribution that your soul expects of you. Your soul has a plan for you; it has an intention and it seeks to fulfill that intention. It needs your help. This perspective means that you have two sources of intentionality: your conscious self and your soul. Tuning in to yourself in a spiritual way means that you can live in harmony with what your soul wants for you. Flow, equanimity and empowerment emerge from that internal harmony.

You give the gift of your actualized self when you develop your talents in harmony with your path. You reveal your life's purpose; you make visible what it is that your soul wants for you.

On the other hand, if you are not on your path, life becomes difficult and filled with one obstacle after another. Enormous efforts yield meagre results. Doors close rather than open. It feels as though the universe is conspiring against you and it becomes dangerously easy to slip into a depressed state through the learned helplessness of your repeated but futile efforts. All of that happens not because the universe is against you, but rather because the universe is trying to help you get back on your right path. It's as though you have wandered off the correct trail and have gotten lost in the brambles, so of course everything is difficult. You become entangled in the underbrush, bloodied and scratched from your struggles to free yourself. The message is not that the world is against you but rather that you need to get back on your path. If you heed the message and do find your path, the situation changes completely. The brambles disappear. Doors open. Opportunities suddenly present themselves, seemingly out of the blue. The people with whom you were meant to be suddenly make an appearance in your life.

Surprisingly, moving from the brambles to the right path can be fairly simple and occur in just a few steps. The tangled underbrush is not far from the clear and easy hiking trail. The path is another brief and easily learned technique that can be taught to anyone including young children.

When you are living in tune with the intention of your soul – your soul's desire – events transpire in a surprisingly effortless way. You are where you are meant to be and that sets things in motion.

There are similarities between the right path and peak performance skills, most notably in the skill of visualizing success. In the right path, you visualize yourself succeeding in being on your path in the future. The right path can be considered spiritual peak performance, with the focus on meaning and purpose rather than on developing skills in sports.

INSTRUCTIONS FOR THE RIGHT PATH

Like peak performance imagery, diaphragmatic breathing and postures, the right path is surprisingly easy to employ and can be learned in just a few minutes. The right path can be used when you are trying to make changes in your life. The changes might be in career, relationships or even deciding where to live. There are three steps.

Visualize Yourself in the Future on Your Path

First, imagine yourself in the future, maybe six months, a year, five years, whatever seems right. In the future, you have found your path; you are doing the thing that you were meant to be doing. What you are doing gives you a sense of meaning and fulfillment in life. You are filled with a sense of purpose and joy. You love what you are doing. It's why you are here on this planet.

Just let the images come up and notice any details. Don't try to make things happen, but rather just observe as the images surface. Try not to be too critical about what emerges – you can analyze at a later time, if you want. Now, though, is the time to just let the images of your path appear and to pay attention to them. No details are too small or inconsequential to be noticed. It doesn't matter if any of it makes any logical sense; it's not a logical method. Your soul has it's own logic.

The process of the first step typically takes about five to fifteen minutes, but can happen in a few seconds. The first, spontaneous images are especially important. It is best when the images appear naturally and freely, as they emanate from a deeper source than your conscious mind. Don't *make* the images happen, *let* them happen and observe. It is helpful to immediately write down everything that comes up and to be as complete as possible. You might keep a journal. You can meditate on these images from time to time, allowing new images to come up and to record them. Often more details emerge over the next week. That's the first step.

Make a Small Step in the Direction of Your Path

The second step involves making a small step in the direction of the path. Ponder the question:

"What's one *small* step that you could make towards being on the path that was identified in the first step?"

Note the emphasis on the smallness of the step. It is not necessary to completely change your life overnight to get on your path. Small steps are OK and will get you there. Examples of small steps:

"I could call the university and see what programs are available."

"I could look on the internet to see if there are any possibilities to work with dolphins."

"I could look at real estate listings to see if I can find a place that looks like that."

Once you have identified one small step, the next action is to simply follow through on making that step. That's your path homework.

Be Amazed

Be amazed emerges spontaneously from completing steps one and two; opportunities open up, people arrive and possibilities suddenly present themselves. You familiarize yourself with the details gleaned in step one, as preparation to recognize the path when it shows itself. That's why a journal is helpful. You can re-read what you visualized and *be amazed* that now you've found it. Otherwise, you could be in the perfect place with exactly the right person, but not recognize it and just walk right by. This way you are prepared. Writing things down is essential as a reminder that the images were there *before* you actually encountered the experience. That will be important information for the skeptical part of your mind.

5
The Phenomena of Anxiety

"What if I'm having a heart attack?"

STUCK IN TRAFFIC

John was driving home from work on a pleasant, sunny afternoon. The traffic was unusually heavy and the driving soon became stop and go. John sat at a light that changed from green to red three times with no movement in the bumper-to-bumper traffic. Finally, the row of cars nudged forward through the light. John noticed that it seemed hot in the car. He was surprised to find he was perspiring heavily. His shirt now clung wetly to his back. He could feel his heart pounding in his chest and he became alarmed, thinking that he might be having a heart attack. He began to gasp for air and he found his airway constricted, as if some unseen foe had him by the throat with an invisible hand squeezing his neck. He felt dizzy and he noticed his hands were trembling. Images of losing control and crashing the car flashed through his mind. He considered abandoning the car on the street and fleeing by foot, but with great effort he was able to maneuver to the first exit and pull off on a side street. He fumbled for his cell phone and dialed 911. In a few minutes an ambulance arrived and transported him to the emergency ward of the nearest hospital. The doctors examined him, ran some tests and told him that physically he was fine. There was nothing wrong with his heart and in fact they thought he was in great shape. They asked him if he was under any stress.

THE POTHOLE

Murray pulled his car out of his suburban driveway and left for work at his usual time of 7:45. He had only driven a few blocks, though, when he began to wonder if he had locked the front door. The thought flitted through his mind like an annoying mosquito and he tried to swat it away but, like a mosquito, it kept buzzing back at him. He fought the impulse to turn around and drive back home to check and see if he had in fact locked the door. He was distracted by these thoughts and so didn't notice a pothole looming up ahead in the street. His car bumped over the hole with a loud bang that riveted his attention back to the task of maneuvering the automobile. All thoughts of checking the front door evaporated.

After a few blocks he started to have an even more worrisome thought. What if he hadn't driven over a pothole but instead had actually hit a child playing in the street? A vivid image of a child's body lying prone and lifeless on the cold pavement darted through his mind, accompanied by a flood of apprehension. After a few more blocks, he could stand it no more and he made a quick U-turn, driving back to where he had been startled by the loud bang.

He scanned the road ahead, dreading what he might find. The street was clear, though, and there were a number of potholes, any one of which might have been the cause of the incident. It was hard to identify the exact place he had felt the impact, but now he was almost all of the way back home and so he felt sure he had passed the spot that caused his alarm. He breathed a sigh of relief; it must have been one of the potholes after all. He turned and headed back to work, now certain to be late in arriving. As he neared his workplace, he had another thought. What if he had hit a child, but the child had managed to crawl off of the street? An image of a child's body lying crumpled and bleeding on a lawn appeared in his mind. He had to go back and check. He drove up and down the street and even went down side streets in case the injured child had managed to crawl that far from the site of the accident, but he could find nothing. Everything seemed to be normal, just another peaceful morning in the suburbs. Eventually he was able to drive all the way to his workplace, now very late because of these delays.

During the day, he found it hard to concentrate on his work. Thoughts of hitting a child on the street kept intruding into his mind in spite of his best efforts to suppress them. He checked the news on his computer several times to see if there was any report of a fatal hit and run in the area. On his lunch hour, he went out to his parking spot and examined the front bumper of his car but nothing seemed amiss.

THAT'S NOT MY HUSBAND

Jarred returned home from his third deployment overseas. He had served once in Bosnia and twice in in Afghanistan. His wife noticed that each time he came home, he was changed by the experience. She confided in a friend that:

"My husband went over there, but that's not my husband who came back."

She noticed that he became increasingly withdrawn and aloof after each deployment. He would spend a lot of time downstairs in the basement and he stopped visiting with friends and family. He had loved going to hockey games but hadn't been to one in years, in spite of many invitations. He was also drinking a lot more, especially in the hours before bedtime. He often came to bed late, long after she had retired for the night. During the night he would toss and turn. Some nights, he would sweat so heavily that they would have to get up to change the sheets. On really bad nights, he would yell out in anger and fear. One night, in his sleep, he punched the pillow beside her head with all his might, as if fighting for his life with some unseen foe. She became afraid to sleep in the same bed with him, so he started to sleep in the spare room.

He rarely ventured out and on those occasions where she could convince him to accompany her to the mall or grocery shopping, he would often leave suddenly, racing out of the building without explanation. She would find him huddled in the car in the parking lot, sunglasses on and baseball cap pulled down low over his eyes.

The family learned to walk on eggshells around him. They became fearful of driving with him because he would fly into a rage over minor incidents. At home, he would be irritable for no apparent reason and he would jump if you approached him from behind when he was not expecting it.

At other times he appeared to be in a daze, as if his mind was somewhere else and he was no longer present in the room. In response to these unnerving experiences his wife learned to gently say his name over and over, telling him he was safe and at home with the family until, eventually, he would again become aware of his surroundings. He never explained where his mind went during these episodes. Watching movies where there were explosions or viewing the evening news would often precipitate the incidents.

PATHWAYS TO ANXIETY

What causes anxiety problems? There is no one single answer as there are a number of possible pathways to having an anxiety disorder. One pathway is genetics. Different people have different constitutions. If you went into a nursery full of infants and popped a balloon, you would see a number of reactions to the sudden sound. Some infants would startle, flinching in response and perhaps crying out in distress. Other infants would barely blink, maintaining a calm composure. They might turn towards the source of the sound in curiosity. The majority, though, would fall somewhere between the two extremes. Everyone has a unique biological constitution that influences his or her response to environmental stimuli. Some are extremely reactive while others are very non-reactive. These differences in the nervous system are noticeable from infancy. Those who have more sensitive and reactive nervous systems are more likely to develop anxiety. It's as if their nervous systems are primed that way.

GENETIC PREDISPOSITIONS

Any parent that has more than one child well knows that kids can have strikingly different personalities right from day one. Some kids love chaos and are comfortable playing in the dirt, hardly noticing that they are covered in mud from head to foot. Other kids like to have everything neat and orderly and would detest playing in the mud. Some kids make friends readily and easily fit into whatever group they are in, while others are shy and timid, reluctant to approach other children. The shyer children tend to pull back from social engagement and avoid rather than explore.

MODELING

How much is genetic and how much is learning? It is difficult to separate the effects of genetics from parental modeling. If you inherited the genetic propensity for anxiety from a parent, then that same anxious person also raised you.

Your caregiver has not only passed on genes, but they have also demonstrated an anxious way of being in the world for you to observe. Modeling is a powerful way of learning and kids are naturally adept in imitating what they see happening around them. Anxious parents not only pass on genes, but they also teach anxiety through example.

OVER PROTECTIVE PARENTING

If your parents had anxiety, they may have developed an over protective style of parenting. If they perceive the world as a threatening and scary place, they will try to protect you from it by encouraging you to avoid things. Don't play sports because you could get hurt. Maybe you should stay home from school because you're feeling a bit tired. Watch out for the glass of milk, you might spill it. Check in with me several times a day so I'll know that you're OK.

There is a difference between healthy parental caution and anxiety. An over protective parenting style means that almost any risk is unacceptable. If you grew up with over protective parents, the messages you got were: the world is a dangerous place; you can't really handle it; and you should avoid risk whenever possible.

ABUSE AND NEGLECT

On the other end of the parenting continuum, a childhood involving abuse and neglect can also be a pathway to anxiety. For example, if your father or mother was an aggressive alcoholic, your family life was likely unpredictable, chaotic and even violent. You learned that you must walk on eggshells, never quite sure what might set things off in a catastrophic way. That is a recipe for anxiety. It really was too much for you, as a small child, to be able to cope with. You learned two negative core beliefs: the world is dangerous; and I can't cope with it. Having a problem with anxiety can be a product of growing up in such a world and having internalized those two beliefs.

If you were sexually abused as a child, your boundaries were violated and as a result, you may not feel that you can say no to things you don't want. You have difficulty setting limits and that makes the world a threatening place.

You might feel a deep sense of betrayal and have problems trusting people so that your relationships become filled with anxiety. You may have difficulty controlling your own emotions and be swept along by intense feelings that overwhelm you. At other times, you might feel numb and disconnected. You have a sense of yourself as powerless in a threatening world.

TRAUMA

Other traumatic events during childhood can also lead to insecurity and anxiety. For example: the loss of a parent or sibling when you were young; periods of separation from your family; being involved in an accident; serious health or medical issues; and moving from one place to another. These can all have an impact on how insecure or anxious you feel later in life.

Traumatic events that happen later in life can also play a role in whether you develop anxiety. Posttraumatic Stress Disorder (PTSD) is the anxiety disorder that is directly linked to the experience of a traumatic event.

ONGOING LIFE STRESS

Ongoing stress can also overtax your nervous system and culminate in anxiety, if that stress is sustained. Examples are: employment in a toxic work environment; having chronic health or medical issues; going through a long and acrimonious separation; and having continuing financial or housing problems. The cumulative effects of the ongoing stress create a chronic state of hyper-arousal in your nervous system that disturbs your sleep and interferes with your ability to concentrate and cope.

PHYSICAL ENVIRONMENTS

Recent research (Lederbogen, et al., 2011) indicates that your brain shows the effects of whether you were raised in the city or in the country. Amazingly, a simple MRI can reveal if you grew up in a rural or urban setting.

If you grew up in the country, your brain and nervous system developed in the rich stimulus world of nature. The sounds, smells and sights of nature comforted you. As a result of that upbringing, you recover faster when you are startled by a sudden loud noise. The small surge of arousal gets rapidly dampened and you quickly return to your pre-startle state of rest. This happens because one part of your brain (the prefrontal cortex) communicates with the part that is sending the arousal (the amygdala) signalling it to calm down. If you grew up in the country these parts of your brain listen to each other. The prefrontal cortex says:

"Don't panic, it's only a loud sound. It's no big deal."

The amygdala hears this and replies:

"OK, good, there's no reason to worry."

This dialogue takes place outside of your conscious awareness. What you notice is a blip of anxiety and then back to your relaxed self.

If you grew up in the city, the calming part of your brain becomes weakened in its ability to comfort the fear part. The calming part gets over-taxed by the constant barrage on the senses that goes along with urban-living. That sensory information could mean the difference between life and death. For example, if you don't look both ways before crossing a street in the city, you could actually die. In the city you are likely to cross the street many times every day. This routine event might not come off as a big deal to your frontal lobes, but it does get the attention of your mid-brain. Even in these seemingly mundane events, your amygdala needs to be vigilant and on guard in order to keep you alive.

Meanwhile, the calming part of your brain goes from one event to the next, always trying to re-set your fear response back to a relaxed state. Eventually, it just gets too much to handle and it can no longer keep up. That part of your prefrontal cortex can lose volume and get smaller as a result; that's what you can see on an MRI. It's as if the calming part says:

"I can't talk to you anymore, you don't listen to me so I'm out of here."

Growing up in the city is one of the root causes for the current pandemic of anxiety in society. The era of anxiety is partially birthed by the proliferation of cities and urban environments. The bombardment of urban sensory noise overwhelms your ability to regulate your threat-alarm responses. These negative effects are compounded by an impoverishment in exposure to nature, with its restorative and healing powers. You drive by nature rather than become a part of it and your nervous system suffers as a result.

The obsessive focus of the media on catastrophic events doesn't help. When you finally do make it home to your place of safety and refuge, the catastrophic events of the day are funnelled into your living room via television and computer.

There are many pathways to anxiety: genetics; personality traits; learning by observation; over protective parenting; childhood abuse and neglect; traumatic experiences; life events; physical environments; and adult experiences. All of these factors can play a role in predisposing you to developing anxiety.

6

The Anxiety Disorders

*"I want to buy a thousand acres
and then live in the middle of it."*

Soldier with PTSD

There are a number of anxiety disorders: separation anxiety; phobias; panic disorder; agoraphobia; social phobia; posttraumatic stress disorder (PTSD); generalized anxiety (GAD); and obsessive-compulsive disorder (OCD).

Anxiety disorders are distinguished from normal anxiety in that an anxiety disorder is extreme and causes significant impairment in your day-to-day functioning. Anxiety disorders also tend to persist over time in a way that normal anxiety does not. Normal anxiety does not impair your life, is less severe and is usually transient rather than long lasting.

SEPARATION ANXIETY

In separation anxiety, you feel anxious whenever you are separated from the important figures in your life. Separation anxiety often occurs after suffering a loss that has made you feel insecure in your attachment to the important people in your life. As a result, you develop an anxious-attachment with those close to you.

Upon separation, you might experience uncomfortable physical symptoms such as upset stomach, headaches or vomiting. You might feel depressed and worry about the safety of the person you are away from. You might imagine catastrophic events happening to them that would result in you never seeing them again.

Separation anxiety can happen in children and in adults. For a child, separation anxiety might mean that you feel anxious when separated from your mother or father. You might cling to them when they are present and follow them around the house in order to stay close to them. If you are home alone and waiting for your parents to return, you might visualize them being killed in an accident and then feel overwhelmed with anxiety.

For an adult, separation anxiety might mean fear of being away from your spouse or some other person of significance to you. You think of the other person constantly and feel apprehensive when they are not available to you. You might worry about the safety of your kids if they are late getting home and repeatedly check on them by phoning or texting them several times a day. This can cause friction in your relationships as they start to feel controlled and monitored.

You may try to avoid separation from the other person by refusing to go to school or by repeatedly checking in on the person when you are away. Separation from the person interferes with your ability to focus on school or work because you are preoccupied with the absent person.

PHOBIAS

Phobias occur in specific situations, such as: fear of heights; dogs; enclosed spaces; dentists; bridges; flying; vomiting; and receiving injections. While most people experience some fear or anxiety in those situations, for a phobia, the anxiety is excessive and unreasonable in the face of the actual level of threat.

Phobias are severe to the point that the anxiety interferes with your normal routines. For example, you might begin to avoid situations that you find distressing and that restricts what you can do in your life. If you develop a fear of heights and bridges, it can limit where and how you travel. You might have to drive the long way around in order to get to your destination because you have to avoid bridges, high places and busy freeways. If you do go near the feared places, your anxiety escalates, perhaps to the extent of having a panic attack.

Phobias can be caused by trauma involving the phobic situation: falling from a high place; nearly choking; having an allergic reaction; being bitten by a dog; or being stung by bees. Phobias can also appear after watching someone else being traumatized in a certain situation. Sometimes there is no obvious history of any trauma related to the development of the phobia. For example, most people have an innate fear of heights and spiders that is likely caused by a genetic predisposition.

The particular fear underlying a phobia is not always obvious. For example, someone can have a flying phobia for a variety of reasons other than a fear of heights or even a fear of the plane crashing. The flight phobia may be a fear of having a panic attack and not being able to leave the situation as you are trapped on the airplane. It could also be a fear of not having any control over the situation as some unseen person is flying the plane. Understanding the nature of the actual fear in the phobia is essential for planning the treatment.

PANIC DISORDER

Panic attacks are brief, but very intense, blasts of anxiety that seem to come out of the blue. They often last only a few minutes but can leave you exhausted and depleted from the sheer intensity of your body's response.

Panic attacks include powerful and distressing physical symptoms such as: heart racing, sweating, trembling, shortness of breath, choking, numbness, nausea, flushing, or dizziness. Sometimes they are accompanied by perceptual changes such as: tunnel vision, feeling unreal, or feeling detached from your self.

Sometimes, when you have a panic attack, you may believe that you are having a heart attack or losing your mind. Those catastrophic thoughts may result in calling an ambulance or going to emergency for help.

In the story 'Stuck in Traffic,' John has a panic attack in his car while waiting for the light to change. He feels trapped in the traffic and unable to escape. The trapped feeling brings on the first physical signs of anxiety in his body. He notices that he is sweating and that his heart is racing, which he interprets, catastrophically, as a heart attack. This catastrophic interpretation of his physical symptoms increases his anxiety, which then spirals into a full-blown panic attack. Now, convinced he is having a heart attack, he calls 911.

Once you have had a number of panic episodes, you are likely to develop a fear that you will have another. You may start to scan for any physical symptoms that suggest a panic attack is about to occur and therefore develop a preoccupation with any physical sensations in your body. You might start to avoid activities that increase your heart rate, such as climbing stairs, having a sauna or going for a run.

You may also become increasingly avoidant of the situations where you experienced panic attacks in the past. For example, if you had a panic episode on a bus or car, you may stop taking buses or driving your car. John is likely to avoid driving in any situation that involves heavy traffic. He might even stop driving all together. His experience in the traffic has been traumatic and so he becomes afraid to go into similar situations. He might become agoraphobic as his world shrinks.

Panic disorder can be thought of as a cumulative stress disorder. Panic attacks often begin when you have been under stress for a number of months. Over time, the stress in your body builds up and eventually overflows into a panic attack. Your system has become so wired that you are unable to get into a relaxed state.

A history of childhood sexual and physical abuse is a risk factor for later developing panic disorder as an adult. It is likely that those childhood stressors affected your nervous system in a way that disturbed the balance between alertness and relaxation, making you more susceptible to developing panic attacks in the face of stressors in later life.

Another pathway to panic disorder is through having a medical problem that mimics the physical sensations of panic. For example, having a hyperactive thyroid can cause panic-like symptoms. As a result, you might develop a fear of your own body's reaction as it creates these blasts of arousal. You first have an anxiety attack in reaction to your body's arousal, but this continues after the medical problem is treated successfully. You become phobic of any arousal sensations in your body and develop a conditioned (automatic) anxiety response to sensations such as heart pounding, sweating and flushed face.

AGORAPHOBIA

In agoraphobia, you develop excessive fear and anxiety related to situations where escaping or leaving may be difficult. For example: being in a crowded restaurant where the way to the exit is impeded would be an extremely difficult situation. Agoraphobia is associated with situations such as: going out of your home, being caught in traffic, standing in line, sitting in a busy theatre or being in a crowd. The fear, though, is not really about crowds or open spaces, but rather about being in situations where you might feel trapped and unable to exit easily; you fear having a panic attack and not being able to get away. If you are away from home, you worry that you will not be able to return home. You may need a 'safe person' to accompany you when you do go out. Sometimes the avoidance can become so pervasive that you become unable to leave your home at all.

Agoraphobia is associated with a childhood involving over protective parents, cold or aloof parenting or separation from a parent. Adult traumas such as being attacked can also precipitate agoraphobia.

SOCIAL PHOBIA

Social phobia manifests in a fear and anxiety about other people. Specifically, social phobia is a *fear of negative evaluation* by others. When you have social phobia, you worry about being judged or embarrassed. You avoid interactions with others if at all possible, especially any interactions where you might be the center of attention. You become preoccupied with what others think of you. You develop ongoing feelings of shame, embarrassment and anxiety, accompanied by low self-esteem. Public speaking anxiety, one of the most common anxieties, is a form of social phobia.

Social anxiety is associated with negative, self-critical thinking. This may be experienced as hearing an internal, critical voice. It's as though you carry with you the voice of an angry and critical parent who continues to berate you and comment on how you are managing things. This negative self-talk only reinforces your low self-esteem.

Social anxiety is more than a normal concern with how you are coming across to others. The anxiety and distress associated with social phobia is severe enough to interfere with the quality of your life. For example, you might avoid activities that you want to do, such as: social gatherings, dating, attending classes, letting others get to know you, or applying for jobs involving social interaction.

Personality traits like shyness, inhibition, and over concern with the evaluation of others can leave you susceptible to having social anxiety later in life. If you were shy as a kid, you are more likely to have social anxiety as an adult, although not every shy kid becomes socially anxious as an adult. Childhood experiences can either moderate or exacerbate those tendencies. A positive childhood upbringing, with safe and secure attachments can modulate the tendencies towards anxiety.

POST-TRAUMATIC STRESS DISORDER (PTSD)

Posttraumatic stress disorder occurs as a result of exposure to an extreme traumatic stressor involving the threat of death or serious injury. If your life is in immediate danger or you are in a situation where you might be physically injured, it is possible to develop PTSD directly from that event. You can also develop PTSD from watching someone else be traumatized.

Some examples of traumatic events are: sexual and physical assault; domestic violence; child abuse; war experiences; imprisonment; car accidents; and natural disasters.

When you develop PTSD subsequent to a stressor, symptoms manifest in four areas: hyper-arousal of the nervous system; re-experiencing the event through memories, flashbacks and nightmares; avoiding reminders of the event; and developing dissociative symptoms such as numbness, feeling unreal, feeling disconnected from yourself or having amnesia for parts of the trauma. These symptoms may occur immediately after the trauma or later on. Often, these symptoms flare up immediately after a trauma, but then naturally fade away over the course of a few days or weeks. If the symptoms persist beyond four weeks, you may have developed PTSD.

Hyper-arousal symptoms involve difficulties with sleep, bouts of irritability, problems with concentration, hyper-vigilance and an increased startle response. In PTSD, the nervous system gets overwhelmed and over-aroused by trauma and so relaxation becomes very difficult. You start to live in a state of over-arousal. The hyper-arousal is accompanied by scanning for signs of threat and becoming hyper-vigilant to potential dangers. You might become very sensitive to loud sounds or crowds, experiencing 'stimulus overload' when there is too much going on at one time.

Re-experiencing symptoms can include recurrent day-time thoughts and images, nightmares, or 'flashbacks', where you feel like you are re-living the event. You may become apprehensive or even try to avoid sleep because of the fear of having nightmares. In the most extreme form of intrusive memories, you may actually feel that you are back in the past, re-living the traumatic event. You can lose touch with your present surroundings as you are caught up in the past trauma.

Stimuli in the environment such as smells, sights or sounds that resemble some aspect of the trauma can 'trigger' a re-experiencing of the trauma. This re-experiencing is different than a normal memory of an event, in that it is much more vivid and intense, as if you were back in the original trauma. These re-living experiences can be extremely distressing, causing you to feel paralyzed and overwhelmed when they occur.

In the story 'That's Not My Husband', Jarred is triggered into re-living his combat experiences by television shows and news stories. He becomes caught up in the past traumas so that he is no longer aware of his present surroundings. His wife speaks to him quietly and repeatedly and is eventually able to help him reorient to his current surroundings. He feels shaken and depleted by these intense experiences and withdraws even more from anxiety, embarrassment and helplessness.

In PTSD, you try to avoid any reminders of the event. Avoidance symptoms may manifest in not talking about what happened, not going near where the event occurred and avoiding any similar situations or triggers. The avoidance can become generalized so that you withdraw from others and become very isolated and reclusive, in contrast with your previous, more outgoing self. Those close to you are often confused and distressed by these seemingly inexplicable changes in your behavior. Jarred becomes extremely aloof and withdrawn from his family members and friends, who are then perplexed and concerned by his behavior.

You may experience emotional detachment in situations where you would normally have some emotional reaction. Instead, you feel disconnected, unemotional and numb. At other times, you feel overwhelmed with feelings; your heart pounds, you sweat and feel panicky. You fluctuate between feeling too much sometimes and then feeling too little at other times.

Depersonalization is a form of disconnection from yourself. Survivors of concentration camps describe feeling disconnected from themselves, as if out of their body. Physically you might feel numb or unreal or that your body has taken on a different size or shape. At times it is as if you are observing yourself from the outside, like you are watching a movie about someone else.

Another dissociative symptom is de-realization, where the world around you seems unreal and unfamiliar. Your perceptions can become distorted, such as: time slowing down, developing tunnel vision or everything going suddenly quiet. These symptoms can be very unsettling and you may feel that you are losing your mind, which only increases your anxiety.

Dissociation can also manifest in amnesia. Parts of the traumatic experience can be wiped out, like a blank piece of the story. The amnesia may occur around the trauma or continue after the event as you begin to have gaps in your daily experience. In PTSD, your memory can become disturbed in a number of ways: by having extremely vivid memories (re-livings) or by having gaps in memory (amnesia).

Not everyone who experiences a traumatic event develops PTSD. The severity/proximity of the trauma is the single most important risk factor. This means that how bad the trauma is (severity) and how close you are to it (proximity) predicts who will get PTSD.

A number of factors can increase the likelihood of developing an anxiety problem in reaction to a traumatic event: the severity of the trauma; how close you were to it; if there were children involved; if you felt in some way responsible; or if you felt helpless to respond. Other vulnerabilities are: having a previous history of traumatic events, having other anxiety problems and having high empathy and high imagery capacity. Any of these can make you more susceptible to developing PTSD in response to a trauma.

GENERALIZED ANXIETY DISORDER (GAD)

GAD is the worrying disorder. Unlike other anxiety problems, the worrying is not limited to specific situations, people, or physical sensations. Instead, there is a worried style of thinking that tends to pervade your mind and is applied to most situations; you worry about whatever is going to happen next. Much of the worry is about routine daily minutia, like whether you will get the kids to school on time, will you have enough time to clean the kitchen and what shirt should you wear. Of course, most people would have some concern with those questions, but, in GAD, they become anxious preoccupations. The worrying persists throughout the day and you may even wake up worrying.

Accompanying the worrying thinking style is a chronic state of muscle tension so that you constantly feel 'on edge'. The protracted nature of these symptoms can leave you with feelings of fatigue and exhaustion, as you get little respite from the worry and the muscular tension.

Another aspect of GAD is difficulty with uncertainty. When you have GAD, you have difficulty in making decisions.

The fear is that you will make the wrong choice. Self-doubt and perfectionism are big parts of GAD. You tend to re-do things because you worry that they are just not quite good enough. This uncertainty can make it hard to move ahead in many areas in your life.

These GAD symptoms tend to be chronic and likely first appeared when you were very young. Personality traits such as inhibition, harm avoidance and worry are associated with an increased risk for GAD later in life. Childhood abuse, neglect or over protectiveness can exacerbate those personality traits.

OBSESSIVE-COMPULSIVE DISORDER (OCD)

Obsessive-compulsive disorder has two primary symptoms: *obsessions*, which are cognitions such as thoughts or images, and *compulsions,* which are behaviors or actions.

Obsessions

Obsessions are intrusive thoughts that typically represent the worst thing that you can think of. The thoughts and images intrude into your mind and cause you to feel horrified and distressed as a result. You try to push the thoughts away, but they keep coming back.

The worst thing that you can imagine will be different for different people. The three main categories of obsessions, though, are: sexual, aggressive and religious.

For example, if you are somewhat sexually repressed, your OCD symptoms may manifest in images of you engaging in some unwanted sexual activity. If you have difficulty expressing anger, you may have aggressive and violent images such as stabbing your wife and children. If you are devoutly religious, you may have thoughts and images of being flatulent in church. The form that the image takes represents the worst thing that you could imagine.

Many people have these catastrophic images but simply dismiss them as weird thoughts. Most people have had the fleeting thought of jumping when standing in a high place. This may have an adaptive function by encouraging you to step back, away from the danger. In OCD, though, you react as if these images represent a real and immediate danger; you get bluffed by the thoughts. You are not really going to stab your wife, jump off the bridge or throw your baby into the traffic, but *what if* you did? You become horrified at the startling images, afraid that they could come true. You do your best to push these terrible images from your mind, but they persist in intruding into your thoughts.

In the story 'The Pothole', Murray has the thought that he has run over a child in the street. This is an example of an aggressive obsessive thought. Murray probably has difficulty expressing anger and so his obsessive thoughts take the form of an aggressive and violent act. He is alarmed by these thoughts and then compulsively checks the road to see if there is a child's body lying on the street. The thoughts stay with him over the day and interfere with his ability to do his job. His obsessions lead to compulsive checking behaviors as he persistently checks the news for any reports of a child injured by a hit and run driver.

Compulsions

Compulsions are ritualized or superstitious behaviors such as counting, washing in a ritualized way or excessive checking of locks or appliances. Not being able to check or wash results in an increase in anxiety. Engaging in the behavior contains the anxiety, at least in the short run. In the long run, though, your anxiety is maintained by the repetition of the compulsive behavior.

Personality traits, such as inhibition and a tendency to excessive negative emotions, are predisposing factors in

OCD. Physical and sexual abuse in childhood and other traumatic childhood events may also predispose you to developing OCD later in life.

THE PREVALENCE OF ANXIETY DISORDERS

	Canada	U.S.
Lifetime	25%	29%
Separation Anxiety	5%	4%
Phobias	8%	9%
Panic	1%	3%
Agoraphobia	1%	5%
Social	7%	7%
GAD	1%	3%
PTSD	7%	8%
OCD	2%	1%

Anxiety disorders are the single most common mental
health problem.

About 50% of those with depression also have anxiety.

Less than 50% with anxiety have been diagnosed.

There are higher rates of anxiety in lower income and
urban dwellers.

7
The Meaning and Treatment of Anxiety

"Pain is inevitable, suffering is optional."

Dalai Lama

THE MEANING OF ALL ANXIETY DISORDERS

In the previous chapter, you have seen how anxiety can be divided up into a number of disorders. This is the psychiatric way of looking at anxiety as a mental health problem with a number of descriptive categories. Defining anxiety problems as disorders means that anxiety is seen as a problem that is somehow different from regular (non-disordered) anxiety. However, another way of looking at anxiety problems is that they are just more extreme or out of balance examples of the same anxiety that everyone experiences as a normal part of life.

At the heart of any anxiety problem is a physiological response to threat. It's the body's way of trying to help you out when you are in danger. It means that anxiety is an adaptive response when there is a real danger.

ANXIETY IN TWO WORDS:

DANGER ➡ ESCAPE

Over time this becomes:

DANGER ➡ AVOID

In anxiety, your mind thinks "danger" and your body responds by giving you arousal to help you flee from the threat. In an anxiety disorder, the *danger* ➡ *escape* connection becomes a chronic way of being in the world.

It is much more adaptive to avoid rather than flee from danger, so avoidance becomes the pattern over time when you have anxiety. It means that you must prepare for possible dangers in advance so that you can then avoid those dangers. This leads to an ongoing and automatic cognitive style (scanning for danger) and body arousal (readiness for flight). Your mind continuously hunts for possible bad stuff that might happen (catastrophic expectations) while your body does its best to help you out by increasing your arousal so that you can get away from the danger ASAP! You start to live as though you are always in some perilous environment; you act and feel as though you are in danger when you are perfectly safe.

ANXIETY IN YOUR FEELINGS, THOUGHTS, ACTIONS AND BODY

Emotions:	Threat, danger, dread, apprehension, panic, foreboding
Cognitions:	"What-if", "yes, but", how can I get out of here?
Behaviours:	Escape and avoid
Body:	Heart pounding, sweating, rapid breathing, adrenalin, glucose

ANXIETY AND TREATMENT

Anxiety disorders are the single most prevalent mental health problem. It is estimated that more than one person in four will have an anxiety problem at some point in their life. However, less than half of all the people with anxiety disorders are ever diagnosed so the prevalence of anxiety is likely much higher.

It is common to hide or cover up anxiety due to shame and embarrassment. Many people suffering with anxiety are reluctant to talk about it or to seek help. Anxiety can be experienced as a personal weakness or failure, especially in a culture where being strong, stoic and fearless is venerated.

The good news is that anxiety disorders are treatable with therapy and with medication. Cognitive-behavioral therapy, in particular, has long been demonstrated to be an effective treatment for anxiety problems. Cognitive-behavioral therapy involves learning techniques to reduce the intensity of anxiety, managing stress more effectively, changing thinking patterns associated with anxiety and challenging the avoidance behaviors that maintain the anxiety over time.

There are a number of other therapies that are also effective for anxiety, including: hypnosis, relaxation, acupuncture, cranial electrical stimulation, massage therapy, meditation and yoga. In the following chapters, common factors in these differing approaches will be outlined in a theoretical explanation as to how such diverse therapies can be effective treatments for anxiety. Understanding and applying these techniques will allow you to master anxiety.

MASTERING ANXIETY

THE A = BCD MODEL

B   C   D

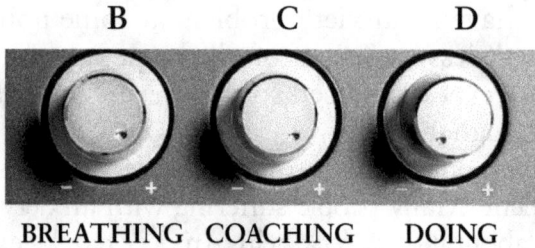

BREATHING COACHING   DOING

Think of **BCD** as being three separate volume controls that play a role in regulating your level of anxiety. Depending on what you do in each one (breathing, coaching and doing) you will either turn your anxiety up or turn it down.

Certain styles of Breathing-Coaching-Doing will crank your anxiety way up, while others will reduce your anxiety considerably. There are gold standards for each of BCD that will help you live in a more relaxed and healthy way.

You can start by identifying your specific BCD elements that result in flare-ups of anxiety and that keep you stuck in the anxiety over time. Do you know exactly what it is that you are doing that turns your anxiety up? When you become aware of the BCD that heightens your anxiety, then you can begin to practice new BCD skills that will instead turn your anxiety down. Over time, these practices will become your new normal. As you rehearse the BCD skills, you become empowered over your emotional states and you learn to master anxiety.

8
Mastering Anxiety Through Breath

"Diaphragmatic breathing is the natural response to the sounds of the ocean."

THE LOST ART OF DIAPHRAGMATIC BREATHING

If you are struggling with anxiety, it is very likely that you have grown accustomed to breathing from the top of your chest. This is not how you were breathing as an infant, when you naturally breathed deeply, from your belly. How is it that your natural skill of healthy breathing has been lost? Part of the answer is that the human environment has changed dramatically over the years. Humans have become immersed in a sensory world of city environments, which are saturated with man-made sounds, smells and sights.

In order to function in that environment, you learn to suppress competing distractions, at least with your conscious mind. Your unconscious mind, however, still encodes the

impinging stimuli, resulting in a chronic level of physiological arousal being held in your body. Your breathing becomes
rapid and shallow, with accompanying movements localized
in the upper torso and chest. Your neck and shoulders tighten
up around the area of this unnatural breathing style. Over
time, this tension develops into neck and shoulder pain. You
go home to relax but there, in your place of refuge, modern
media thrusts all the catastrophic events of the world literally
into your face. It's no wonder that the present era has been
called the age of anxiety.

Diaphragmatic breathing is an innate, biological
response to the soothing sounds, sights and smells of nature.
It is the natural physical response of your body to the sound
of the ocean waves; the smells of the sea; the call of the birds
flying overhead; and the wind rustling through the trees.
That world has been replaced with a world that is largely
human-made, with its own unnatural and disturbing stimuli.
The new sensory envelope increases arousal in your nervous
system through a surge of sympathetic activity.

The experience of peaceful immersion in nature modulates your nervous system and directs a restorative shift
of state from one of arousal (sympathetic nervous system
activity) to relaxation (parasympathetic system). The resulting state of tranquility is essential for stress management,
immune response, healing and rejuvenation.

Nature shifts your state and soothes your physiological
being, inducing feelings of tranquility and peacefulness. The
raw stimulus of nature calms and stabilizes your heart rate;
your blood pressure lessens and your breathing naturally deepens. You are of the earth and it is your sensory connection
with the earth that sustains and nurtures you. Nature induces
diaphragmatic breathing and with the loss of communion with
nature comes the loss of diaphragmatic breathing.

Fortunately, diaphragmatic breathing can be re-learned
and brought back under your control. The goal is to teach

your body to breathe diaphragmatically automatically, as a customary and ongoing way of breathing. In other words, you can teach your body to breathe diaphragmatically all the time. The advantages are many: reduced anxiety; lowered stress; enhanced immune functioning; maximal performance; and greater resilience. These are just a few of the many extraordinary benefits of diaphragmatic breathing.

ANXIOUS BREATHING: HOW TO TURN THE VOLUME UP

Anxious breathing is localized primarily in your upper chest and can be described as chest breathing. Your shoulders, neck and upper back get recruited to help out with this breathing and over time you develop tightness and aches and pains in those areas. Your shoulders hurt and anxiety literally gives you a pain in the neck.

Anxious breathing is shallow, rapid, gasping-type breathing. This may alternate with repeatedly holding your breath or hyperventilating. This type of breathing rockets your heart rate up and pumps your blood pressure through the roof. Anxious breathing increases sympathetic arousal. The problem is that you are neither breathing deeply enough, nor holding the air in your lungs long enough, for the oxygen to be absorbed. As a result, your heart has to work overtime to compensate. Your level of arousal soars. Heart pounding, tight chest, can't catch your breath: sound familiar?

DIAPHRAGMATIC BREATHING:
THE GOLD STANDARD FOR BREATHING

Any slow, deep breathing is good for you and will help to lower your anxiety. The gold standard, though, is called *diaphragmatic breathing* and detailed instructions for this have been given earlier. This is the ideal that you want to work towards. Diaphragmatic breathing is taught in a number of contexts:

yoga; meditation; sports; for singers; and for musicians playing wind instruments. However, diaphragmatic breathing
can become your natural way of breathing all of the time
and not just employed on specific occasions. Diaphragmatic
breathing is associated with relaxation but you can breathe
this way even when you are running. Elite athletes learn this
skill in order to improve their athletic performance.

Diaphragmatic breathing is also called belly breathing.
When you breathe diaphragmatically, your belly pushes out
as you breathe in and then moves in as you breathe out. Your
shoulders and upper chest remain perfectly still and relaxed,
as the movement of your breathing is concentrated in your
abdomen. Good posture and maintaining a straight spine is
conducive to diaphragmatic breathing. It is easiest to practice
when you are lying prone on your back.

This type of breathing dramatically lowers your heart
rate and blood pressure. You shift into a relaxed, parasympathetic state as you continue to breathe this way. You might
start to yawn and your stomach might start to gurgle as
blood flow returns to your internal organs. The muscles in
your face relax, causing you to look younger and even more
attractive than usual. You feel more and more comfortable
and relaxed. Imagine how you will feel when you teach your
body to breathe like that all the time!

Diaphragmatic breathing helps your body get into a
state of relaxation associated with parasympathetic nervous
system activity. Other therapies such as hypnosis, yoga, relaxation, meditation and massage also help to put you into that
parasympathetic state. Being in that state is naturally healing. It is the state that enhances relaxation, rejuvenation, restoration and replenishment in both the body and the mind.

9
Mastering Anxiety Through Self-Coaching

*"The greatest weapon against stress is our ability
to choose one thought over another."*

William James

THE NATURE OF COACHING

What is coaching? Coaching, whether good or bad, shows up in three ways in your cognitions: styles of thinking, core beliefs, and images. These cognitive events each play a role in how you end up feeling about yourself and impact on your ability to do things in life. Coaching is how you talk to yourself: will it be encouraging and helpful, or self-limiting and fear inducing? Will you spur yourself on to new and greater achievements or will you stop yourself in your tracks?

SELF-MONITORING

In order to change your thinking patterns, you first have to become *aware* of them. Self-monitoring helps you to make the connection between your thinking and your anxiety. Self-monitoring represents the ability to observe yourself: to notice what you are thinking and imagining. Then, you can target key areas for change and develop specific strategies to counter your particular style of anxious thinking. Anxious cognition is all about danger and threat so self-monitoring means that you identify your specific danger thoughts.

Notice any thoughts and images that go through your mind just before your anxiety escalates. Those moments are fertile ground for discovering the specific cognitions that are playing a role in your anxiety. Use any spike in your anxiety as a reminder to pay attention to what just went through your mind. Those thoughts are often fleeting and almost subliminal. Your attention is likely to be more focused on the feeling of anxiety rather than on your cognitions, so any anxious thoughts and images can disappear without notice, unless you are deliberately making an effort at self-monitoring.

First, you become aware of what you are doing to make yourself more anxious, and then you can plan new and more helpful coaching strategies. There are a number of ways that coaching can increase your anxiety, but it all has to do with the idea of danger.

ANXIOUS COACHING

Anxiety, in two words, is: *danger* ➡ *escape*. So, any time you have thoughts and images of *danger* flash through your mind, you turn your anxiety volume up. What happens when you focus your attention on threat? Your mind repeatedly calls out: DANGER! DANGER! Your amygdala, deep in your mid-brain, hears the alarm and responds by saying:

"OK, if there's danger out there, I'll help you out by turning your arousal way up so you can escape! Let's get your heart rate up, here's some adrenalin – that will help –

and let's get you sweating right now because you're really going to heat up when you're fleeing from the danger!"

The resulting escalation in anxiety can happen even when you are sitting safely at your desk at work, lying in your bed or walking home. If your mind thinks DANGER, your body will respond with increased arousal. You don't need a real, external danger. All you need is the idea of danger.

Danger thoughts result in increased arousal in your body and this may happen many times throughout the day. It's like turning the BCD volume dials up again and again, each time you think of danger or threat. It's exhausting and unpleasant. The more you turn the anxiety up the easier it gets because, with repetition, you are creating pathways in your brain that become highly efficient at raising your anxiety level.

Anxious coaching can manifest in styles of thinking, negative core beliefs and in catastrophic imagery.

ANXIOUS STYLES OF THINKING

Styles of thinking are repetitive patterns of thought. Some examples of anxious styles of thinking are: catastrophic expectations (what-if); discounting positive things (yes-but); always preparing for the worst; self-critical thinking; black and white thinking; extreme thinking; personalizing things; over estimating the probability of bad things; dwelling on the negative; and focusing on the past or future at the expense of the present.

What-If?

What-if and *yes-but* are two of the most common styles of thinking associated with anxiety. If you have anxiety, it is almost certain that you are engaged in what-if and yes-but thinking. What-if... is about the future while yes, but... is about the past. Both have a negative and self-limiting effect.

What-if and yes-but are examples of *scanning* and *discounting* that maintain the anxious core belief that you live in a dangerous world.

In what-if thinking, you are constantly predicting the bad stuff that might happen:

"What if the plane crashes?"

"What if I'm having a heart attack?"

"What if they think I'm a loser?"

"What if I screw this all up?"

"What if I'm trapped and can't leave?"

"What if she says no?"

"What if she says yes?"

"What if I go to the group and they all laugh at me?"

"What if I have a panic attack?"

"What if I'm stuck in traffic on the highway?"

"What if I get lost?"

The possibilities are endless, limited only by your imagination and you know how well that works. In what-if, you scan for potential disaster. Your mind focuses on the possibility of things going very, very badly. As a result, you may fail to enjoy, or even notice, the genuine positive things in life, because you are so preoccupied with possible threat. That takes away from the quality of your life and inhibits your joy in living.

What-if is a way of keeping your guard up at all times. It becomes difficult for you to ever relax. You may even start to think of relaxation itself as dangerous. It is as though if you let your guard down for a moment, you may not see the bad stuff coming. Your vigilance keeps you in a chronic state of sympathetic arousal and with an over abundance of stress hormones coursing through your system in preparation for escape.

Yes, but...

Yes-but is the style of thinking that discounts positive events. *Yes*, something good happened, *but* it doesn't count because...

This keeps you stuck in the anxiety, even when you begin to make small steps ahead in your recovery. You overlook and discount the things that you are doing well. It becomes difficult to see the way out of the anxiety:

"Yes, I found the group helpful, but I don't think it will work for my kind of anxiety."

"Yes, I got the promotion, but now they will want me to work longer hours."

"Yes, I gave a presentation without any anxiety, but I was on medication."

"Yes, I drove on the highway, but my husband was with me."

"Yes, I haven't had a panic attack for weeks, but I haven't been going out much."

"Yes, it worked this time, but what if it doesn't help next time?"

Yes-but is a recipe for maintaining anxiety. It becomes difficult for you to absorb the genuine positive things that are happening when your attention is repeatedly redirected back to potential or imagined negatives. It *discounts* the positive, leaving you mired in the anxiety. You ignore your gains and instead place your attention on what might be missing. In peak performance you learn to notice and acknowledge what you did well in order to improve your game even further. The yes-but style of discounting makes that impossible.

Yes, but can be associated with a fear of letting your guard down. If you have been living with anxiety for some time, it might feel dangerous to relax. It's as though you are walking through a minefield and so you need to maintain your hyper-vigilance to threat in order to survive. You may have developed a phobia for relaxation, which itself now seems dangerous. In that case, you are operating from underlying core beliefs that direct you to:

"Always be prepared for danger, never let your guard down."

"Relaxation is dangerous!"
"Watch out so that you see the next bad stuff coming!"
"If you're not ready, you'll get clobbered."

Self-Critical Thinking

Self-critical thinking means that you often berate yourself. You find fault with what you have done and you discount your accomplishments. This style of thinking often emerges from a history of being repeatedly criticized by some else. Maybe you grew up with a critical adult who often put you down, using a harsh or sarcastic tone of voice. Over time, you internalized that negative critic to the point where you no longer need them to be present, because now you carry the self-berating voice around with you. In some ways, that's even worse than the outer critic, because now it's inescapable: wherever you go, there you are. This constant critical companion keeps your anxiety going 24/7. It's like someone following you around, looking over your shoulder and continuously putting you down. Imagine how stressful that would be! Well, it has the same effect when you do it to yourself; your body tenses up, you feel anxious and you become *less* able to do things. You start to doubt yourself and, over time, the self-critical thinking becomes a self-fulfilling prophecy.

Black and white thinking

Do you tend to see things as either black or white? Is life a pass or fail event? Is it all or nothing? If so, you tend to think in extremes. Life is rarely this unambiguous; it's usually a mix of some things that went well and others that did not go as well. In retrospect, even some of the things that did not go as well often turn out to be opportunities for learning and growth. When you think in a black and white way, you lose a lot of useful information. You over simplify things:

"I really blew that talk. I was nervous at the beginning."

"I'm sure I failed the exam. I left one of the questions blank."

"They didn't like me."

"I only got an A *minus!*"

Excessive Obligation and Duty:
Meet the Should's and the Have-To's

The style of thinking associated with an over-active sense of obligation and duty is evident in the frequent use of the words *should* and *have to*:

"I should be able to do this."

"I have to help out whenever asked."

"I should always be on time."

"I should be happy."

"I have to try harder."

When you use should, it often means:

"I should, but I won't be able to, therefore I'm failing and in fact I'm a failure as a person."

Should is accompanied by feelings of guilt and failure. If these feelings are familiar to you, notice how often you use should and have to. It indicates that you have a negative core belief related to obligation and that belief is playing a role in perpetuating your anxiety. This style of thinking leaves you feeling like a failure in life and that you need to try harder, which leads to more pressure and more anxiety. You should be doing more but you're not. What's wrong with you?

Living in the Past and the Future

Another style of thinking associated with anxiety is to focus on the past and future, at the expense of the present. You ruminate over what just happened and find fault in how you handled things. You go over the events of the past day with a critical eye, finding inadequacies in what you said or did. You think of what you could have done differently, reinforcing a sense of failure and not being good enough.

Looking ahead, you expect disaster in the future. You feel that you have to plan everything out so that you are prepared for all eventualities. You wake up with your mind racing as you go over the upcoming days event in an effort to foresee any potential problems. These preoccupations mean that you are not engaged in the present experience and as a result it is hard to fully enjoy whatever you are doing in the here and now. Instead, you worry.

CATASTROPHIC IMAGERY

Coaching is not only about the content of your thoughts; it's also about the images that go through your mind. Images can be just as important as thoughts in determining your level of anxiety.

People vary in their ability to create mental pictures. Some people are blessed with a capacity for extremely vivid imagery. Those people tend to be creative; often they are artists. They have excellent imaginations and can visualize things almost as clearly as though those things were real. For example, a musician might hear a composition in his head and then simply write down the music, thus creating a musical work. Another artist might visualize a painting or a sculpture, which then becomes the inspiration for her art.

If you are blessed with the ability to generate vivid imagery, this talent can make your anxiety worse. Imagine for a moment having the thought: *what if the plane crashes?* Now, imagine being able to see, hear and feel that experience with great clarity and vividness. All of your senses become involved. Visualizing the look of terror on your co-passengers faces as they realize you are all about to die; hearing the sound of the motor exploding into flames as the wing is ripped away from the fuselage; experiencing the feeling in the pit of your stomach as you are plummeting through the air; and... well, you get the picture. If you have vivid imagery, perhaps your heart rate increased and you started to sweat as you were reading this description. That's your mind turning up the anxiety in your body through the use of catastrophic imagery.

Visualizing is a powerful way of communicating DANGER! DANGER! to your brain. It is like showing a movie to your amygdala and the movie just happens to be a horror flick!

Catastrophic images will increase your anxiety exponentially. A picture is worth a thousand words in turning your anxiety up and even more so when you have excellent imagery ability.

NEGATIVE CORE BELIEFS: GHOSTS OF THE PAST

Core beliefs, or schema, are underlying beliefs about yourself and the world. Everyone has core beliefs, some negative and some positive. They are a central part of human information processing; they allow you to readily understand the world around you and serve to direct your actions in the world. Core beliefs allow you to process information in a rapid and effortless way as they provide you with a ready-made explanation for understanding whatever is happening. They act as a lens from which you view your experience and imbue meaning in the events that occur in your life. Core beliefs are prescriptive; they tell you what to do based on the nature of the belief. For example, a core belief that the world is a dangerous and unpredictable place, might result in the rule:

"Never let your guard down."

Core beliefs come from your past and represent things that you have learned. If your past was stressful, these core beliefs are likely to be negative. Take a moment to review the three stories (Anne, Beth and Warren) in the prologue of this book and notice the core beliefs that came out of their childhood experiences.

"I'm invisible."
"I'm an outsider, I don't belong."
"I will fail."
"I don't matter."
"People can't be trusted."
"Bad things will happen to me."
"Don't draw attention to yourself."
"Always keep busy."
"Never let anyone down".
"Always be nice." "Never upset anyone."
"Always fit in."
"What others think of me is the most important thing."

Core beliefs are self-perpetuating through the cognitive processes of scanning and discounting. Remember what-if and yes-but? They are a product of underlying negative core beliefs. You scan for what you believe and you discount infor- mation that contradicts that belief. For example, if you have a core belief that you are a failure as a person, you will scan for evidence to confirm that belief and discount information that contradicts it. You notice how you are coming up short and minimize your successes.

If you believe that people can't be trusted, you will look for examples that prove your point:

"You see, it's just what I thought all along, people can't be trusted!"

If someone does appear to be trustworthy, this will be discounted in a yes, but... style of thinking:

"Sure, he helped out, but it's probably just because he wanted something!"

This confirms your pre-existing bias and further cements the belief. Core beliefs then become self-fulfilling prophecies. They're tenacious.

Core beliefs operate outside of your conscious awareness but the effects are visibly noticeable. Whenever you have
strong negative emotions, there is an underlying core belief
that has been activated. It is helpful to notice what thoughts
are going through your mind whenever you start to have a
strong emotional reaction. You can use self-monitoring to
identify your core beliefs.

The Role of Core Beliefs in Negative Emotions

Negative core beliefs are the source of intense negative emotions. Whenever you have the experience of suddenly feeling
really bad, you can suspect that a negative core belief has
been activated. It is not the situation that caused the bad feelings, but it is your *interpretation* of the situation that results
in the negative emotional state. Your pre-existing core belief
gets evoked in the situation, provides the meaning to what
just happened and then you feel badly as a result.

Like the saying: wherever you go, there you are; wherever you go, there your core beliefs are. You interpret what
is happening to you in the present through the filter of the
core belief from the past. Those interpretations then evoke
the negative feelings.

For example, you are out happily shopping in a mall
when you see someone that you work with in your office.
Naturally, you smile and say hello. To your surprise, though,
your colleague ignores you completely and walks right by
without even acknowledging your presence. You stand there,
immobilized, watching her walk away. Suddenly, you feel
worthless. A deep sense of despair wells up inside of you.
You were in a good mood just a minute ago, but now you
are feeling down and depressed. What's going on? Did the
actions of your co-worker cause your feelings?

Viewing these events from a cognitive model, the
actions of your co-worker evoked your pre-existing core

belief and it is that belief that stirred up the negative feelings. Any time you have strong negative feelings, it is a sign that some negative core belief has been activated. This is an excellent time to self-monitor: how were you thinking about your co-worker walking by? Maybe you interpreted the situation this way:

"I am not even important enough to say hello to."

"I'm invisible and worthless."

"I don't matter at all."

Feelings of worthlessness and unimportance make sense in light of these interpretations. However, these thoughts actually reflect an underlying core belief (I don't matter) that you learned at some time in your past. The ghost of the past gets summoned in the mall as your co-worker walks by and appears to snub you. In your past, you were treated in a way that made you believe you didn't matter and you internalized that belief about yourself. The present situation with the co-worker evokes that old core belief and results in feelings of worthlessness and despair. It is the core belief that causes the emotional reaction, not the situation.

Later, you return to work and you ask the co-worker about her behaviour. She apologizes and tells you that she had just got off the phone after receiving some very bad news. She was worried and preoccupied with the news and so hadn't noticed you. It turns out that her behaviour had absolutely nothing to do with you and everything to do with her.

DEVELOPING POSITIVE STYLES OF THINKING

Now that you've identified some of the ways you might be coaching yourself into more anxiety, what can you do about it? How can you coach yourself in a more positive and helpful way, one that helps you master your anxiety and be fully present in your life?

Compassionate, Encouraging and Positive Self-talk

Good coaching means positive, realistic and encouraging self-talk. You are being a good coach when you speak to your self in a kind and compassionate way. Think of a young boy or girl who is feeling frightened and overwhelmed. What would you say to that scared child in order to help him or her? You would likely be encouraging and positive. It would help for the child to know that you are on his side and that he's not alone:

"Listen, you're going to be OK and I am going to help you. Just take a nice deep breath. You can do this. Remember when you did this before? You did just fine then and you're going to be all right now too. Take your time. You know you don't have to do it all at once; just do what you can. I'm here with you. You're going to be OK. I know you can do this. I believe in you."

You intuitively know what would work to soothe and comfort a scared child. However, you may be using a less helpful strategy when you talk to yourself; you may be criticising and berating yourself. This has the opposite effect to what is desired because self-critical, angry or pressured self-talk turns the anxiety up, not down. Bullying yourself through the anxiety makes the experience even more stressful. On the other hand, encouragement, patience and understanding turn the anxiety volume down. Repetition and persistence in using positive self-talk over time are important. That frightened child doesn't stop being frightened right away; it takes a little time and encouragement. Persistence is important.

Encouraging Tone of Voice

Your tone of voice is as important as your words. When comforting a scared child, you would naturally use a compassionate, reassuring tone of voice, a tone that reflects calmness, patience, support and encouragement. It's meant to be soothing, so speak slowly, with confidence and warmth, using simple and positive words. Use a lot of repetition. The tone of your voice (even in thoughts) is a powerful form of communication so the child listening to you would start to relax and not feel so overwhelmed. You have the same effect on yourself when you use compassionate self-coaching.

Take a slow and relaxed diaphragmatic breath. On the exhalation of breath, use a positive, encouraging tone of voice and say:

"You are going to be OK."

Another intake of breath and then on the exhale:

"Just take your time, I know you can do it."

Another inhalation of breath, and:

"I'm with you, you're going to do just fine."

You can practice this out loud and, at other times, just to yourself. Link the positive coaching to your exhalation of breath even when you are just thinking the words. This will help you to shift into diaphragmatic breathing and a more relaxed state of mind. Shifting your body towards a more parasympathetic state enhances the positive effects of the coaching. Do this a hundred times over the next few weeks. Notice how you are starting to do this naturally as a new way of coaching yourself.

Positive Language

It is important to use positive language when coaching yourself. For example, think about this attempt at self-coaching:

"I'm sure that the plane will not crash and explode. We will not all die a horrible and fiery death!"

The problem with this style of self-coaching is that catastrophic thoughts and images are embedded in the thoughts. Your unconscious mind tunes into:

"Crash...explode...die? What! That can't be good! I have to get out of here now!"

So, instead, practice using positive language and imagery. Take a diaphragmatic breath and say:

"The plane will soon land smoothly and my friends will be happy to greet me at the airport. Now, I can feel the plane touching down; it's a nice soft landing! Then we disembark and I'm so happy to have arrived. The air smells good! I'm excited to see my friends. It's a beautiful sunny day. My friends are waiting for me and they are smiling and waving when they see me. Now they are giving me a big hug! It's so good to see them!"

This self-talk is done using a positive and encouraging tone of voice and the images are all positive. Notice that there are only positive words and so your unconscious mind hears: friends... happy.... nice... good... excited... beautiful... smiling... hug. You practice this style of coaching and then, when you do land and greet your friends, your prediction comes true. This reassures your unconscious mind, and your anxiety is reduced. Imagine predicting positive, realistic outcomes and then have them come true, hundreds of times. You master anxiety with this positive way of coaching yourself.

Realistic Thinking

It is important to be positive, but also realistic in your thinking. Using language that accurately describes the situation in a positive light will be easily accepted by your unconscious mind. In the above example, it is very probable that the plane will land smoothly and that your friends will be happy to see you. However, telling yourself that you absolutely won't experience any turbulence on the flight is probably less realistic, as some turbulence is expected on most flights. Realistic, rather than unreasonably optimistic thinking helps by reinforcing your thinking when the predicted events come true.

CHANGING COGNITIVE STYLES

Change 'Should' to 'Want'

When you notice that you are using the words *should* or *have-to*, try replacing them with *want to*. For example, you notice that you are having this thought:

"I should stay home this afternoon and clean out the garage."

Changing the should to want to, results in:

"I want to stay home this afternoon and clean out the garage."

Now take a moment to ponder the truth of the statement. Do you really want to do that? Maybe you do:

"If I finally clean out the garage I can park the car inside and it will feel like a real accomplishment."

In this case you discover that you really do want to clean the garage and so you do it with a positive attitude. You look forward to the final results. Maybe you celebrate by going out for dinner. Job well done!

Maybe you decide that you really don't want to clean the garage out at all, it's simply a sense of obligation. I really don't want to, but I should because I have these beliefs:

"Always do whatever work needs to be done."

"Never leave anything half done."

"Always finish what you start."

"Get the work done first, before you do anything else."

However, after considering the question, what you really want to do is to go for a bike ride and enjoy this beautiful sunny day. If that is your answer, use this situation as an opportunity to challenge the old dysfunctional beliefs. Tune in to yourself and respect what it is that you truly want. Go for the bike ride. Enjoy the beautiful day. Tolerate some guilt and do it anyway. Practice positive coaching while you are at it.

Either way, when you decide what it is that you truly

want, you honor and respect yourself when you act on that desire. Your actions emerge from your intention and that is an essential part of empowerment. You are less likely to feel resentful because you are being true to yourself, rather than operating on a self-induced guilt trip. Even if you clean up the garage, you enjoy the result.

Change Yes-but to Yes.

If you notice that you are using *yes-but*, put a period after the *yes* part. For example:

"Yes, I did well on the test, but it was easy and I studied for hours. Other people probably did better than me without working at all. Why do I have to work so hard compared with others? I must be dumb."

Change this by putting a period after the yes part:

"Yes, I did well on the test. Period."

Now, restate the yes part. Elaborate it. Dwell on the positive.

"Yes, I did do well on the test. In fact, I got an A+. I really aced that exam! I am proud of doing so well. I studied hard and I got a very good mark as a result. Yay!"

Notice the very different end-points involved in the two trajectories. Focusing on the *yes* helps you to build on genuine positives. That's a peak performance skill. Change yes-but to yes-period one hundred times. Notice that now you are thinking differently automatically.

Change What-If to Imagine Success

In anxiety, *what-if* is followed by negative and catastrophic expectations:

"What if I fail? What if I get rejected?"

Change what-if to focus on positive outcomes. Keep the what-if, but add a positive expectation. Use what-if to imagine success:

"What if I do really well? What if other people are welcoming and accepting?"

Use encouraging words to follow what-if. This is also an excellent opportunity to practice peak performance imagery; enhance your positive anticipations through visualization.

Peak performance imagery is imagery that depicts the most successful outcome that you can imagine. In sports, elite athletes use this type of imagery in order to improve their performance and gain an advantage over their competitors. Having the mental edge is a huge benefit in elite sports where physical skill levels are so similar that differences are measured in microseconds. Imagery gives the athlete that edge and it will benefit you as well.

How does peak performance imagery work? The high diver, just before her dive, closes her eyes and takes a diaphragmatic breath. Then she visualizes a perfect performance; she sees and feels each movement of her upcoming dive in vivid detail. She uses imagery because she has learned that a picture is worth a thousand words in communicating to her unconscious mind. Visualizing success is a powerful and rapid way of letting her unconscious mind know what she would like to happen next. It's the opposite of anxiety imagery; instead of predicting disaster, she visualizes success. The imagery guides her performance, her body follows her mind and she does her best dive ever. That's the peak in peak performance and imagery helped it all to happen.

Olympic athletes are more likely to win a medal when they use imagery to enhance their performance. However, peak performance imagery can benefit everyone, not just elite athletes. Imagery is an important part of self-coaching and can be used as a tool in your daily endeavours. Visualizing success in the future and recalling successful past experiences will diminish your anxiety while enhancing your performance and skills. It results in feelings of mastery.

In the same way that you trained your body to breathe instinctively from the diaphragm, the ultimate goal here is to have your mind naturally visualize peak performance experiences. You will need to practice imagining and recalling success in a number of situations; as you persist in creating positive imagery over time, your mind will spontaneously begin to think in a peak performance way.

Peak Performance Imagery Exercise

Take a moment right now to begin this practice. First, consider what you will be doing for the rest of the day. It doesn't have to be some big event; it might just be an everyday activity. Maybe you will go for a walk. Maybe you will have dinner with your spouse.

Take a nice diaphragmatic breath and close your eyes. That shifts your state and helps your unconscious mind to be even more receptive. If you are going to go out to dinner with your spouse, visualize that dinner going extremely well. Make it the best dinner you can possibly imagine. Where are you sitting? What does the room look like? How is the food? Can you see the smile on your wife's face as she leans forward, fully engaged in the conversation with you? The words you are speaking are less important than the overall feel of what is taking place. The dinner is going amazingly well. It's the peak performance of dinner with your spouse. After it's over, on the way home, you feel content and you smile with satisfaction because it went so well.

This visualization may take only a few moments. It's not the length of the exercise that matters; it's the quality of how much you can bring it alive and view the scene in all its positive and vibrant glory. Briefer and more focused practice is preferable to longer efforts where your attention wanders. Practice the visualization from between thirty seconds and a few minutes. Start using peak performance imagery everyday for the next two weeks. As a result of that repeated practice, this new imagery will become your natural way of thinking, just as positive and encouraging self-talk will become your spontaneous inner voice.

DEVELOPING POSITIVE CORE BELIEFS: MASTERING THE GHOSTS OF THE PAST

Self-Monitoring and Core Beliefs

The first step in transforming negative core beliefs is to recognize them. In the Appendix, there is a self-monitoring form (situation-thoughts-emotions) that will help you to identify your core beliefs. You can use this form to keep a journal of moments where you end up feeling bad. For example, you might feel anxious, angry, sad, despairing, hurt, helpless or hopeless. Any of these negative feelings can signal that a core belief has been activated. It is important to fill out the form as soon as possible when you are having the negative feelings; otherwise, it's difficult to remember what you were thinking at the time. Often these thoughts are almost subliminal, taking place in the back of your mind while the intense emotions are front and center.

Situation

Under the *situation* section of the self-monitoring form, describe the situation you were in just prior to the emergence of the negative feelings. This is simply a description of the facts of what was happening, without any interpretation or judgement:

"I said hello to a co-worker and she walked right by me."
"I was walking my dog."
"I was asking my son to put the dishes away."
"I was driving and I missed my turn."

Emotions

The second part of the form that you fill out is the *emotions* section. What did you end up feeling in that situation? There might be more than one feeling. List them all:
"Hopeless and suicidal."
"Useless."
"Anxious."
"Angry."
"Scared."

Thoughts

The first two sections of the form are the easiest to fill out. It's usually obvious what the situation was and how you ended up feeling. The *thoughts* that flitted through your mind can be a little harder to identify. What were you thinking about the situation? How did you interpret the situation in a way that resulted in the emotions? Did you have images?

It's important to list all the thoughts and images that went through your mind at the time. These thoughts can occur fleetingly, just below conscious awareness, at a pre-conscious level. It might take a little exploration before you can identify an underlying core belief.

Some examples of negative core beliefs are:
"I'm worthless."
"I'm invisible."
"I don't matter."
"I'm not important."
"Don't trust anyone."
"People will be mean."
"I'm on my own."

When a negative core belief gets activated in the present, the experience is a familiar one, like:

"That's the story of my life."

These beliefs reflect past experiences where you were badly treated or neglected. Those experiences caused you to believe something negative about yourself or your lot in life. The beliefs are about your past, but they intrude into your present; that is the nature of core beliefs. Once you have identified the negative core belief, you can write a new one, as if you are reprogramming your brain.

IDENTIFYING A NEW CORE BELIEF

Ask yourself these questions: What would be a more helpful, healthier belief than the old, dysfunctional one? What core belief would I want my children to have? Sometimes it's simply the opposite of the old belief:

"I am worthwhile."

"I do matter."

Sometimes it's more balanced. The old, negative core beliefs are often extreme in nature:

"I don't matter at all."

"I'm completely worthless."

A more balanced and less extreme belief might be:

"I matter as much as anyone else."

"I am just as worthwhile as others."

Once you have articulated a new core belief, you can use both cognitive and behavioural strategies to transform your old belief into the new one. It's as if you have created a new software program that you want to input into your unconscious mind to overwrite the old, dysfunctional programming.

Following is an example of using the self-monitoring form to identify the old negative core belief and to create a healthier new one.

EXAMPLE OF USING SELF-MONITORING FORM

Situation:	Saw co-worker in the mall and they walked by me without saying hello.
Emotions:	Worthless, Shocked, Sad, Despair
Thoughts:	I'm invisible. I don't matter. I'm nothing. What's the point?
Positive Thoughts:	Maybe something is going on with them. I hope they're OK. I am worthwhile.

COGNITIVE STRATEGIES FOR TRANSFORMING NEGATIVE CORE BELIEFS

Type your new belief into your cell phone as a screen saver. Every time you use your phone, the new belief appears in your visual field. Take a moment to read it to yourself. Take a diaphragmatic inhalation of breath and read the new belief on the exhalation of your breath, using a slow, confident tone of voice:

"I do matter. I am worthwhile."

The old belief has been operating in your unconscious mind for many years. In order to re-write it, you will need to practice having the new belief in your mind at least several times a day. Reading the new belief only takes a matter of seconds; it's a small, but vital investment in your time. Repetition is important. The number one rule for change is this: in order to change an old pattern, you have to repeatedly do something different than what you were doing before. Repeatedly having the new thought is doing something different.

It is very helpful to use a confident and clear tone of voice when you read the card. Don't rush. Slow down, take a nice diaphragmatic breath and then read the card with conviction. Read it to yourself and also out loud, when appropriate. Do this several times a day for two weeks. Notice how you start to believe the new thought.

Now that you have been practicing cognitive change, it's time to tackle behaviour change. This means that you are going to *do* something different. What could you do differently in this case?

BEHAVIORAL STRATEGIES FOR TRANSFORMING NEGATIVE CORE BELIEFS

Take some time to visualize yourself going through the upcoming day, from when you get up in the morning to when you go to bed at night. Only this time, imagine yourself going through the day and you truly believe, on a deep level, the new and healthier belief. For example, if you truly believed that you do matter and that you are a worthwhile person, what would you do differently tomorrow? Watch yourself going through the day with this new belief and notice any changes. These could be just small alterations in what you do. In fact, small changes are good; that's where you want to start. Once you have identified what you would do differently, based on the new core belief, take a moment to write down these new behaviors:

"I guess if I believed I mattered, I would eat better. I'd have a better breakfast."

"If I believed I was worthwhile, I would actually take a coffee break at work instead of just working through the day. I might go out for a walk at noon instead of working over my lunch hour."

Now you have a plan for specific behavioural changes that will reinforce the new and more helpful belief and overwrite the old, dysfunctional one. Practice these small changes every day for the next two weeks. Continue to read the card several times a day while you practice the new behaviors. It doesn't take that long to re-write a core belief, but it does take focus, persistence and repetition. The focus comes from practicing the precise thoughts and behaviors that you have identified. It means you practice specific examples of the new positive belief; that's how you target the old belief for change. Repetition and persistence means you practice several times a day for a few weeks.

10
Mastering Anxiety Through Changing What You Do

*"Full engagement and participation is
the gold standard for exposure therapy."*

AVOIDANCE IS THE BEHAVIOUR OF ANXIETY

A voidance and anxiety go hand in hand. In fact, avoidance *is* the behaviour of anxiety; it's what anxiety is all about. Any time you avoid something, your anxiety gets reinforced. That means it becomes more entrenched. When you avoid things because of anxiety, you can expect increased anxiety in the future. In the immediate moment, though, your anxiety goes down because you have left (escaped) the fearful situation:

"Phew, that was close, but I got out of there! What a relief!"

The reduction in anxiety on leaving the situation confirms the danger:

"My anxiety went down when I got out of there, so it must have been really dangerous!"

Your anxiety drops when you leave the situation

because it has served its purpose. It gave you the arousal to help you flee from the situation and now that you are out of the situation, the arousal is no longer needed. It's done its job. Unfortunately, the accompanying reduction in anxiety acts as a big reward for leaving and so *leaving* gets reinforced. The payoff is that it feels good to get rid of the anxiety. All intro psych students learn this basic law of learning: behaviour that gets reinforced gets repeated. It means that when you avoid and your anxiety drops, your avoidance increases. Avoidance maintains anxiety. Your world shrinks as a result.

Some avoidance is obvious and some is not so obvious. These types of avoidance can be called overt and covert avoidance. It is important to become aware of both types of avoidance related to your anxiety.

Overt Avoidance

Sometimes you are well aware that you are avoiding something. For example: not taking the bus; avoiding driving on the freeway; not going to the store; not getting into the elevator; and not showing up to work on a day where you have to present at a meeting. These avoidance behaviors are obvious and overt; you know full well that you are avoiding those situations. However, not all avoidances are immediately apparent. Some are quite subtle and, as far as you know, you are not avoiding anything.

Covert Avoidance

Covert avoidance can be thought of as secret or hidden avoidance. It is avoidance that is not so obvious. You might not avoid the situation itself, but you hold back from being fully present when you are in the situation. You don't fully engage, even though you're present.

You go to the group meeting but you don't make eye contact with the other group members. Instead, you keep your gaze downwards towards the floor while you imagine other group members looking at you disapprovingly. You go to your classroom, but you never ask a question. You slump in your chair, hoping not to be noticed and called upon by the teacher. You force yourself to get on the airplane, but you avoid looking out the window. Instead, you sit in the aisle seat, tightly gripping the armrest and looking down at your feet. You avoid any conversation with your fellow passenger.

Distraction is another form of covert avoidance. It might help you get through the immediate situation but in the end, it only reinforces and sustains your anxiety. You desperately think of something else so you don't notice that you are in the situation; you become preoccupied and not fully in the experience. You listen to music on your headphones while you are driving on the freeway. You count in your head as you walk by the graveyard.

Covert anxiety undermines the therapeutic effects of exposure therapy. It stops you from getting better, even when you repeatedly expose yourself to the feared situation. That's why recognizing covert avoidance is an important part of mastering your anxiety. Identifying your covert avoidance will help you to plan and structure your exposure therapy.

EXPOSURE IS THE OPPOSITE OF AVOIDANCE

Exposure therapy is the behavioural therapy for anxiety. It involves facing your fears directly; that means going into the very situations that are making you anxious. It is usually the last thing that you want to do. You might even be skeptical about the benefits of exposure therapy:

"Are you sure this is a good idea? Isn't it better to just avoid the whole thing?"

Exposure is thought to be essential in recovering from any and all anxiety problems. Every treatment for anxiety has at least some element of exposure therapy. Facing your fears helps you to develop a sense of mastery in the situation. You master something by fully engaging in it.

READINESS FOR EXPOSURE THERAPY

Timing is important. You need to be ready to do exposure therapy. If you are overwhelmed with emotions and flashbacks of traumatic memories from the past, you may not be ready to do the exposure work quite yet. First, you may have to deal with the past issues and learn how to get into a relaxed state on a regular basis, so that you are feeling stronger and more ready to handle the exposure part of the therapy.

The preceding chapters on managing your states and emotions provided you with the skills you will need to prepare for the work of facing your fears. It is wise to master diaphragmatic breathing and positive, encouraging coaching before you engage in challenging exposure work; those skills will help to make your exposure work easier and less stressful. You will use those skills to decrease your anxiety while you are in the situations that you have been avoiding. That will help you to develop a sense of mastery and empowerment, as your world expands and you gain a sense of comfortableness in going into previously avoided places.

TYPES OF EXPOSURE THERAPY

There are different forms of exposure therapy: systematic desensitization and flooding therapy.

Systematic Desensitization

Systematic desensitization is a kinder and gentler approach to exposure therapy, although it is also probably slower than flooding. In systematic desensitization, you methodically set small goals and then increase the challenges as you build successes over time.

EXPOSURE THERAPY IS SUCCESSFUL
WHEN YOUR ANXIETY DROPS
WHILE YOU ARE STILL IN THE SITUATION

This:

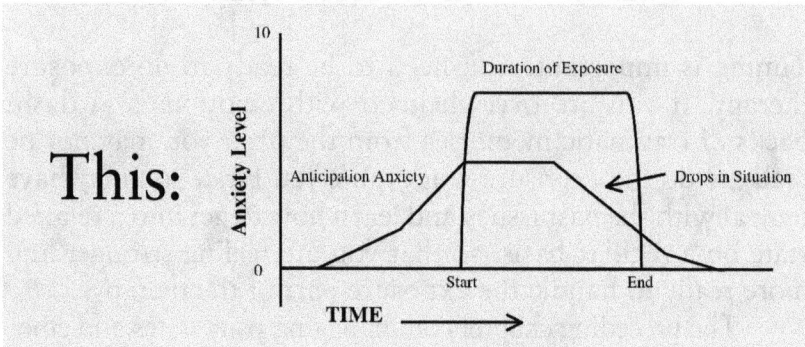

Not
This:

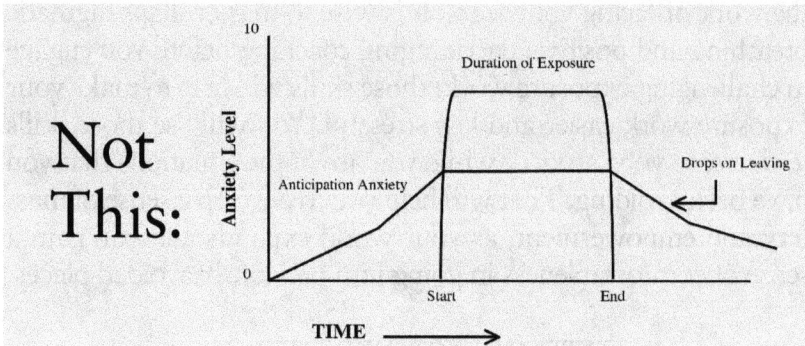

STAY IN THE SITUATION UNTIL
YOUR ANXIETY COMES DOWN

For all forms of exposure therapy, the frequency and duration of your exposure are important considerations. It is essential that you stay in the situation long enough to feel your anxiety come down. That is a key part of any exposure work. For example, if you were mall-phobic and went into a mall, but then hurried through to the far exit and left, it is likely that your anxiety would drop only *after* you exited the mall.

That's bad. You want your anxiety to drop while you are *in* the situation. Instead of hurrying through the mall, it would be more helpful to go into the mall, find a quiet spot to sit and stay there for some time. Practice your diaphragmatic breathing. Coach yourself in a positive and encouraging way. As you are feeling more comfortable, wander around a little. Then, when you truly feel your anxiety has dropped, you can leave. It is crucial to feel your anxiety decreasing considerably while you are still in the situation; that's how you will know that your exposure therapy is working.

Frequency of exposure is another important consideration. If you get on an airplane or give a speech only once a year, you are unlikely to get much reduction in your anxiety. Your exposure isn't frequent enough to have much effect. Joining a public speaking group and giving a talk every week would be much more helpful. Longer durations and greater frequency of exposure accelerate the positive effects.

In systematic desensitization, you evaluate the difficulty level of the challenge. If your goal is too difficult to start with, break it down into more manageable steps. What will help you succeed? Does going with a friend help to make it easier? Does the time of day matter? What if it's less crowded? Is a close friend easier than a stranger? Is having a friend over for dinner easier than going out to a restaurant?

Start by rating your goals on difficulty level from one to ten, with ten being extremely different and one being something you already are doing with only minimal anxiety. A rating of five represents a moderate difficulty level; it's definitely challenging, but you could do it if you pushed yourself out of your comfort zone.

Don't start with a difficulty level of above five. You are less likely to have a good experience of your exposure work. Remember that if your anxiety only comes down when you leave the situation, that's actually counter-productive. What you are aiming for is a decrease in anxiety while you are in the situation. Set things up to make that happen; stack the deck in favour of yourself succeeding. In order to have a successful exposure experience, consider the variables involved that will make it easier or more difficult.

Following is an example of breaking a driving phobia down into smaller steps that are more likely to result in success. That entails developing a graded hierarchy for doing systematic desensitization: what will make it easier and what will make it more challenging?

A man with a driving phobia identifies these variables: it is easier for him to drive on a side street rather than on a highway; it is easier when his spouse is with him than when he is alone; it is easier on a weekend morning with less traffic, rather than in rush hour.

The plan he develops is that he starts on a side street, on a quiet morning, but without his wife present, in order to make the step a little more challenging. He already drives on the side street with his wife and he wants to push himself a little, beyond his comfort zone. He plans his frequency and duration as driving every morning for seven days, for at least twenty minutes. Then, as he becomes comfortable with that scenario, he will raise the bar by driving on a highway, in a non-busy time, with his spouse. Each step is mastered until the step of driving on a busy highway without the spouse is attempted. The development of feelings of mastery in the previous steps means that his final step is not nearly so daunting. He has learned to feel confident in his ability so that what had originally been a ten in difficulty is now only moderately challenging; maybe it's rated as a three.

The following example gives an illustration of how he created a graded hierarchy of difficulty in order to structure his exposure therapy in a step-wise fashion.

CREATING A HIERARCHY FOR GRADED EXPOSURE
(Breaking Goals Down Into Manageable Steps)

10 *(Most Difficult)*	*Driving on a busy highway in rush hour by myself*
9	
8	*Driving on a busy highway, with my spouse*
7	*Driving alone on a highway, early morning*
6	
5 *(Moderate)*	*Driving on highway early morning on a Sunday, with my spouse*
4	
3	*Driving on a side street, early morning on a weekend, by myself*
2	*Driving on a side street, early morning on a weekend, with my spouse*
1 *(Easy, I do it now)*	

Starting Goal: *(Set goal in the 3-5 difficulty range).*

*Driving on a side street,
early morning on a weekend, by myself.
I will do this for seven days,
each time for at least twenty minutes.*

FLOODING

In the flooding model of exposure therapy, you immerse your self in the situation. You jump into the deep end of the exposure pool and you learn to swim more quickly as a result. For example, you ride in the feared confines of an elevator, going up and down for hours, until eventually you are bored. You get in your car and drive on a busy highway for a number of hours. You stay on the roller coaster all afternoon. Flooding can be a more stressful and intense approach to exposure therapy, but it's also more rapid in promoting desensitization. It is helpful if you master the skills of breathing and coaching in easier situations first, as they will help you benefit more rapidly from a flooding approach. The skills you learn in the systematic approach are transferable to the flooding method.

Some situations, like flight phobias, lend themselves more readily to a flooding model of exposure. It is more difficult to break down an airplane flight into smaller steps; once you're on the plane, you're committed for the duration. How motivated you are to overcome your anxiety quickly is also a factor in considering whether to use a flooding approach in your exposure work.

Albert had a panic attack while driving on a major thoroughfare. He drove on the highway daily to get to his office, as it was the shortest and fastest route. Since having the panic attack, though, he avoided the route entirely and instead took a series of side streets to make his way to and from work. This new route was very inconvenient and took more than twice as long as the highway. Because of that inconvenience, he was very motivated to overcome his anxiety. He was afraid, though, that he would have another panic attack if he got back on the highway; after all, that's where the last one happened.

Albert decided to try a flooding approach to exposure therapy. He made sure he had a full tank of gas and got onto the freeway early in the morning. The plan was to drive the full length of the highway through the city, back and forth, until his anxiety was eliminated. He would stop only when he was bored.

His anxiety increased slightly as he approached the spot where he had the panic attack, but dissipated as he drove by. He was more preoccupied with the long hours of driving ahead of him rather than worrying about that one spot. When he got to the other end of the city, he turned around and drove back. The traffic grew heavier as the morning progressed but he was also becoming increasingly comfortable with the road and so his anxiety stayed at a low level. After a few hours of this back and forth driving, he decided that he was now bored and so he could end the exposure therapy. To make sure he was bored and not just talking himself into another avoidance (he had self-monitored that cognitive pattern in the past), he decided to drive one more back and forth. Doing so convinced him that he was indeed bored and not rationalizing. He drove home with no anxiety, but with a strong sense of accomplishment. The following day, he used the highway to get to his workplace and he has continued to do so with no anxiety.

COMBINING SYSTEMATIC DESENSITIZATION AND FLOODING

You may choose to do flooding exposure in situations that don't lend themselves well to a more gradual approach. For example, you might have a driving anxiety and a bridge phobia. You have become more comfortable driving on the road from your systematic desensitization work, but still find any high bridges to be quite anxiety provoking. You drive over the bridge but your anxiety only goes down at the end of the bridge, which takes a minute to cross. The duration is not long enough to really do the work. You plan your flooding therapy by walking over the bridge and staying on it until you are bored. Then you drive repeatedly over the bridge taking the next exit to return in a loop-like fashion over and over, until you are bored with the bridge.

DESENSITIZATION VS. SELF-EFFICACY

One result of practicing exposure therapy is desensitization; your body becomes less reactive to the feared situations with repeated exposures. Your heart stops beating so hard, your breathing deepens and you become more relaxed. You gain a sense of comfortableness in the situation arising from the repeated exposures. Eventually the once stressful situations become as comfortable as any other situation since your body doesn't react with heightened arousal to being in the situation. That's desensitization.

Beyond the objective of physical desensitization, though, is the idea of efficacy. It means that you develop a sense of mastery and confidence in your ability to take on challenges. Efficacy is a much more significant goal than simple desensitization. Through efficacy, you develop empowerment. You don't just learn to tolerate situations, but to fully engage and even enjoy being in those situations. You gain self-confidence as you grow and evolve from your experiences.

MAXIMIZING THE EFFECTS OF EXPOSURE THERAPY

Is simply being in the situation enough to bring your anxiety volume down? The answer is: not necessarily. Remember the discussion of covert avoidance? Covert avoidance undermines the positive effects of exposure. Fortunately, there is a way to practice the exposure therapy that overcomes those effects. It represents the gold standard for doing exposure therapy.

Diaphragmatic breathing was identified as being the gold standard for breathing. Encouraging, positive self-talk is the gold standard for coaching. The gold standard for exposure therapy is full participation and engagement in the situation.

Full Participation and Engagement

Full participation and engagement in the situation is the gold standard for exposure therapy. Just going into the situation repeatedly is sometimes not enough. If you want to bring your full game to the exposure therapy, surrender to being there. Don't hold back in any way; participate fully and completely. For example, if you have social anxiety and are in a group, don't look at the floor. Instead, make eye contact with other group members. Talk about yourself and share some of your experiences with the group. If you are giving a formal presentation, don't hide behind a podium or read from notes as a way of avoiding being there. Instead, walk towards the audience. Open your arms as if embracing them, look out at the smiling faces and say to them:

"I'm so glad to be here with you today."

That's participation: surrendering to being where you are; full exposure; no avoidance behaviours; and no holding back. Yes, it's probably the last thing in the world that you want to do, but it is also the single most powerful skill that you can engage in mastering your anxiety. Full participation, without holding back, turns the anxiety down in a way that you likely have never imagined possible. It's the gold standard for exposure therapy.

It also means that you apply the BC in the D. Breathe deeply, visualize yourself succeeding in being there before you enter the situation and coach yourself in a positive and encouraging way. Then, fully engage in the situation.

Changing Covert Avoidance to Full Participation

Joanne, a secretary in a large and busy office, suffered most of her life from social anxiety. At work, she would become anxious whenever she had to take notes for the staff meeting. Unfortunately, this meeting took place weekly in the staff boardroom and the nature of her job required her to attend each one. Every week, she would not sleep well on the night before the meeting; she would worry obsessively and she would feel sick to her stomach. This unpleasant situation had been going on for several years. She had considered quitting her job, but other than the meeting, she enjoyed her work and it provided a good income. She felt trapped.

Joanne's strategy to minimize her anxiety was that she would avoid talking to other staff members before the meeting, in the hopes that they wouldn't expect her to speak during the meeting itself. When they all adjourned to the boardroom, she would pick the seat nearest the door. She would hold her writing pad up in front of her so that others could not see her hand shake when she was taking the minutes. She frequently looked down at her notepad during the meeting and avoided making eye contact with other staff members. She would glance repeatedly at the clock and the door. The hour seemed to go on forever. She would think:

"When is this going to be over? Why is it taking so long?"

Sometimes she would see herself running out of the meeting and even fleeing from the building. Her heart would pound in her chest when these images went through her mind. She always toughed it out though, staying for the entire meeting and faithfully taking notes for the minutes.

On a scale of one to ten, her anxiety stayed at an eight during the meeting and it had been that way for several years. Her naturally occurring exposure therapy – going into these weekly meetings and staying for an hour – seemed to have no effect whatsoever on decreasing her anxiety over the years. What is going on in this situation? Why isn't her anxiety getting better with all the exposure therapy? How was she holding back from fully being present in the meeting?

Joanne was able to identify her covert avoidance: not speaking with the other staff; looking down; glancing at the clock; hiding behind her notepad; and sitting by the door.

She was also able to identify her escape thoughts and images and made the connection between these images and her heart pounding.

Armed with those insights into her covert avoidance, she approached her next meeting in an entirely different way. She spoke to her colleagues prior to the meeting. They discussed how the weekend had been and exchanged pleasantries about grandchildren and gardening. Joanne barely noticed when they adjourned to the boardroom as she was engaged in making small talk. She did remember to sit away from the door with her back to the clock. She started to raise her notepad, but then thought better of it and placed it flat on the table in front of her. She made eye contact with others and, as she suspected, they engaged her in conversation when she did so. She had moments when she wanted to turn and look at the clock but she determinedly refused to give in to those impulses. She was amazed when the meeting suddenly ended; it had seemed to only go on for minutes. It was the fastest hour-long meeting she had ever experienced in all her years of work.

On the scale of one to ten, she reported that her anxiety had been.... zero! She had no anxiety in the meeting at all, after suffering for several years with debilitating apprehension and fear.

Even though Joanne repeatedly exposed herself to the feared situation over many years, she held back from being fully present and engaged in the situation. Her behaviors and thoughts were instead concerned with escape and avoidance. As a result of that preoccupation, her intense anxiety persisted. Once she fully engaged in the situation, her anxiety disappeared. Covert avoidance keeps anxiety going, while engagement in the situation diminishes the anxiety. If you are staying and participating, there is no need for heightened arousal to help you flee from the situation.

EXPOSURE THERAPY AND THE ANXIETY DISORDERS

Your avoidance behaviors will vary, depending on the nature of the particular anxiety problem that you are facing. You can apply your exposure therapy by targeting the specific situations that you find to be the most challenging.

SEPARATION ANXIETY

If you have separation anxiety, you try to avoid situations where you are apart from the other person. When you are away from them, you might repeatedly check on them by phone, email or text.

Your exposure therapy would therefore involve being away from the person, while fully engaging in whatever situation that you are in. You would also decrease and eventually eliminate any checking behaviors, so that you could tolerate longer periods of time being away from the person.

If you have had a loss that has caused the separation anxiety, it is important to take the time to grieve that loss. It is best to do that grief work before you tackle the exposure therapy. It is important to do exposure therapy in a thoughtful and considered way, with an awareness of any complicating factors. The chapter on empowered parenting gives a case example of treating separation anxiety that was successful because of an awareness of the subtleties in what was transpiring in the interaction between mother and daughter.

PHOBIAS

In phobias, your exposure work is directed at the specific situation that you are avoiding. For example, you may be avoiding dogs, high places or bridges. You carry out your exposure therapy by going into those situations gradually, so that you become more comfortable with each step. If you have a dog phobia, you might begin with a picture of a puppy. Then, as you become more desensitized to the picture, you would go into a room with a real puppy. In that way you gradually increase your exposure while gaining a sense of mastery in each step. Systematic desensitization is very well suited for the treatment of most phobias.

Blood Phobia

In blood phobia, there is a fear of getting needles or listening to discussions of medical procedures. The sight of blood or images of surgery results in intense anxiety and feelings of wooziness. In blood phobia, you may experience a drop in your blood pressure, unlike other anxiety problems where your blood pressure goes up. As a result of the drop in blood pressure, you may actually faint. If you have a history of fainting at the sight of blood, you first need to learn how not to faint, before you do the exposure therapy.

This is how you can prevent yourself from fainting:

On the first signs of feeling faint, fist your hands near your stomach while tightening your arms and chest, as though you were a bodybuilder posing for a picture. The muscular tension acts in the same way that a pressure suit helps a pilot to not pass out when under large gravitational forces. The pressure suit stops blood pressure from dropping too rapidly by externally applying pressure to the circulatory system. That keeps the blood in your head and so you don't lose consciousness.

Once you have confidence that you can stop yourself from passing out, you can begin your exposure therapy.

PANIC DISORDER

In panic disorder, the targets for exposure may not be as obvious. You might be avoiding situations where you previously had a panic attack. If you had a panic attack in your car during rush hour traffic, then you might avoid driving in heavy traffic. If you had a panic on a bus, you may stop using the bus for transportation. However, in panic disorder, you also become afraid of the panic itself. You become fearful of your own body, especially any feelings that are similar to the sensations of panic, like: heart racing, flushed face, sweating, and trembling. Just noticing those sensations in your body can result in anxiety. That is why you might have a paradoxical reaction to relaxation training.

A Paradoxical Reaction to Relaxation

If your anxiety unexpectedly increases during a relaxation exercise, you are having a paradoxical reaction. Why are you getting more anxious when you are trying to relax, rather than becoming calmer? Relaxation exercises often start by having you close your eyes and focus in on your body. You might become aware of your breathing and of your heart beating. In panic disorder, those may be the very things that alarm you, because they have been the signal that you are starting to have a panic attack. That's exactly what you have been trying to avoid. So, when you put your attention on your body, you start to feel more anxious instead of less anxious.

You may have been trying to avoid any physical sensations of arousal such as sweating, heart racing, shallow breathing or flushed face. You may have stopped exercising, walking up stairs or going to the sauna.

Exposure therapy for panic means that you go into those situations that evoke your feared physical sensations. You might go to the gym and run on the treadmill. You might go into the sauna where you sweat and feel the heat. You deliberately evoke the feared sensations in order to desensitize them. In panic disorder, relaxation training can become part of the exposure therapy so that you desensitize to your normal physical sensations. You can break down your exposure therapy into manageable steps with the skills you learned in systematic desensitization.

Fear of Fear: Learning to be Afraid of Your Body

Certain types of anxiety in particular exemplify the idea of anxiety as being a fear of fear. Panic disorder and health anxiety are two such instances. In both of those anxiety problems, you become afraid of your own body's fear reaction. Any unusual physical sensations become cause for alarm.

An Escalating Spiral of Anxiety

Panic attacks usually start with a physical symptom of anxiety: heart racing, sweating, flushed face or a feeling of dizziness. This is followed by a catastrophic interpretation:

"Oh no, I'm having a heart attack!"

"Maybe I'm going crazy and losing my mind!"

If these interpretations are correct, the situation is pretty bad indeed. Therefore your body reacts to these DANGER thoughts by increasing your arousal to help you flee the situation. Unfortunately, that means even more heart racing, more sweating and more vertigo. Then, the catastrophic thought:

"Oh no, it's really happening! I *am* having a heart attack!"

Then there is even more arousal and so the panic attack becomes full-blown. This escalating spiral of anxiety emerges from the interplay between catastrophic thoughts and physical sensations. It all happens quickly and almost subliminally, so that you may not be fully aware of the catastrophic thoughts as the intense physical symptoms hijack your attention.

Overwhelmed by the intense physical sensations, you may go to the hospital by ambulance (remember John stuck in the bumper-to-bumper traffic), convinced that you are having a heart attack or that you are going crazy. As a result, you might start to avoid anything that could bring on those symptoms, such as going to the gym or climbing a flight of stairs.

In health anxiety, you become preoccupied with health concerns and worry that you are developing some catastrophic illness. You focus excessively on physical sensations such as tightness in the chest, sweating, dizziness, nausea or other aches and pains. You begin to notice every twinge and ache and you constantly scan your body for any unusual physical sensation that could suggest you have some dire illness. You might start researching various ailments to see what possible catastrophic illness you might be contracting. What-if... thinking runs rampant and reassurance works only briefly to quell your anxiety, then it's back to the worry.

In both these types of anxiety, you develop a fear of your own body and its natural responses. Physical sensations result in a rapid spike of anxiety. What can you do to desensitize your fear of fear? One powerful tool for desensitizing these physical reactions is called radical acceptance.

"You cannot change anything unless you accept it."

C. G. Jung

Radical Acceptance

Radical acceptance means that, instead of fearing your physical sensations, you welcome and embrace them. This is usually the last thing that you feel like doing when you are having anxiety. You've been busy doing everything you can to get rid of the anxiety, not accept it. In radical acceptance, you fully welcome the sensations. The radical part means that you accept the feelings fully, completely and without reservation. For example, if your heart was pounding in your chest, you could practice radical acceptance by placing your attention directly on the sensation. Then you would coach yourself by completely accepting and welcoming the feeling of your heart racing:

"Wow, I have such a powerful heart muscle! I can really feel it beat in such a powerful and strong way! Thank God I have such a great heart muscle! It's like I'm Superman/Superwoman! Thank you to my heart! I can even see myself going over to my heart and giving it a big hug and a smooch and I'll tell it what a wonderful job it's doing! Thank you to my heart!"

This represents a radical departure from catastrophic thoughts around the possibility of impending heart attacks and insanity. Instead the symptoms are welcomed and even embraced. Humour and exaggeration are helpful tools. When you radically accept your symptoms, you are no longer adding more fear to the mix and so your anxiety drops rather than soars.

Radical acceptance of your physical symptoms is a powerful technique but it can be challenging to do, in light of years of fear and aversion to those sensations. However, if you are able to engage in radical acceptance, your physical sensations diminish rapidly.

AGORAPHOBIA

If your panic disorder has evolved into agoraphobia, there are specific locations and situations that you have been avoiding. For example, in the story: Stuck in Traffic, John had a panic attack in his car when stuck in heavy traffic. He became afraid that he was having a heart attack and that he would lose control of his car. He felt trapped and his fear actually brought on the panic attack in an escalating spiral of anxiety.

John started avoiding situations involving heavy traffic after that experience. Therefore, his exposure therapy would involve driving in traffic. He might start out by driving on a normally busy highway, but at a time when traffic is light.

Then, as he felt increasingly confident he could increase the difficulty of the situation.

John would also identify other locations he might be avoiding, such as crowded restaurants, sitting away from the aisle during a movie or going into crowds. In these situations, the way to the exit is not clear and free and he thinks:

"What if I have a panic attack and I can't leave?"

In order to break your exposure therapy into steps, you might start by sitting a few seats in from the aisle. Then, over time, you would work your way into the middle of a crowded theatre until you felt comfortable doing that. You would practice your coaching and breathing while you are in the situation:

"I am going to be fine. This is a good place for me to practice diaphragmatic breathing. I am going to stay and feel more relaxed. I am proud of myself for doing this today."

If you have both panic and agoraphobia, master the panic first, then go into the agoraphobic situations. Practice the skills of deep-breathing, positive self-coaching, relaxing and radical acceptance until you are no longer having panic attacks. Then bring those skills into the avoided situations.

SOCIAL ANXIETY

In social anxiety, the avoidance involves people. The fear is not of being attacked by people, but rather of being judged in a negative way. This fear of negative evaluation can cause you to avoid intimacy in your relationships. You don't say what you truly feel and think in order to avoid the anticipated judgement from others. Exposure therapy means that you start to express yourself more openly. You can think of it as exposure to intimacy. You might start with the person with whom you feel safest and practice opening up to them first, until you begin to feel comfortable doing so. Then, you could be more open with other friends and family members that you trust.

Practice the coaching and breathing when going into social situations. Visualize yourself being comfortable and open with others. Use a positive, encouraging and compassionate way of coaching yourself. Remind yourself:

"I have a right to be here."

"I am just as valuable as anyone else."

Have these thoughts a hundred times.

POSTTRAUMATIC STRESS DISORDER

In PTSD, the avoidances are related to situations that remind you of the trauma. In car accidents, you might avoid driving. In war experiences, you might avoid driving by parked cars, loud sounds, crowds, or certain ethnic groups. In sexual abuse, you might avoid situations where you are physically touched. Sometimes the avoidance is very generalized so that you become aloof and reclusive, avoiding all social contact. A soldier once said to me:

"I'd like to buy a thousand acres and live in the middle of it!"

If you go into very remote areas you will find an over representation of people suffering from PTSD. Their avoidance is extreme. They have withdrawn from humanity and hide away from the rest of society as a way of coping with their symptoms.

There are different phases to PTSD treatment. In the first phase you learn to reduce the overwhelming hyperarousal, through practicing various techniques such as relaxation, meditation, yoga or massage. Once the hyperarousal is decreased, you then talk about what happened (trauma processing therapy) so that you can work through the parts of the trauma that are haunting you. When the memories of the traumatic experience are diminished, then you can begin to challenge the avoidance behaviour through exposure therapy. If you are overwhelmed with flashbacks and nightmares, it is not yet the time to do the exposure work.

When you are ready to challenge your avoidance behaviors, it is helpful to confront them in a step-wise fashion. The goal is to attain a sense of mastery in the feared situations. Approaching challenges in a gradual way is more likely to be successful than simply plunging in to the most difficult situation. For example, if you have been sexually abused and are uncomfortable being touched, you might go to a massage therapist, but only have a shoulder massage while sitting up. You would leave your shirt on and the massage therapist would agree to not block the way to the exit. Then, as you became increasingly comfortable with that situation, you could receive the massage therapy by lying down.

It is important to consider whether you feel ready to take on any particular step of the exposure therapy. The more control you have, the better. If you push yourself too much, you can have an increase in your anxiety and then revert to avoiding and that's counter-productive. Instead, choose situations where you are likely to win the battle and gain a sense of mastery. Flexibility in exposure therapy helps so that you can adjust the degree of difficulty as you carry out the various levels of challenge. You can't win them all, but start winning some.

OBSESSIVE-COMPULSIVE DISORDER

In OCD, challenging any related compulsive behaviors augments the exposure therapy. If you worry that you haven't locked the door (the obsession) and then repeatedly check the door afterwards (the compulsion), the exposure therapy would be to lock the door and then stop checking.

It is helpful to become fully aware of what is going through your mind when you are locking the door. With

OCD, you are likely distracted when locking the door, thinking:

"Well, I can always come back and check it later."

Because you are distracted, you are not fully present and aware of locking the door. Later, when you ask yourself whether the door is locked or not, you don't have a clear memory of locking it, so you go back to check it to reassure yourself. As you check, though, you might be thinking that you can come back later to re-check.

You need to do something differently in order to get a different outcome. When you lock the door, focus your attention completely on what you are doing. Be fully present in the moment; feel your hand on the doorknob, pull the door and feel how it doesn't come open because it is locked. Take a deep breath and practice good coaching by telling yourself, in a firm and confident voice:

"It is locked. I can feel that it's locked. Yes, I have locked the door."

Later, when the urge to check comes up, you will be able to access a clear memory that you have locked the door:

"No, I don't need to check. It is locked. I can clearly remember the feeling of my hand on the doorknob. Yes, it is locked."

The memory is easily accessible because you vividly encoded the experience while locking the door. Reaffirming that experience helps you overcome the urge to check.

GENERALIZED ANXIETY DISORDER (GAD)

In GAD, the anxiety is generalized rather than being specific to a certain situation. You become preoccupied with the near future and you worry about whatever is going to happen next. You ruminate over upcoming events and plan for anything that could possibly go wrong. You agonize over decisions; it feels as though making the wrong choice will result in catastrophic consequences. Whatever you decide, you second-guess yourself afterwards.

The targets for exposure in GAD are less obvious than in phobias and social anxiety. One focus for exposure therapy in GAD involves making decisions. You might go into a store find a shirt you like and just buy it without equivocating. You might choose a restaurant, a meal from the menu, a show to watch on TV or any one of a hundred small decisions you make during the day. You would act decisively, tolerate some anxiety and abide by your decision.

Another target for exposure in GAD is that of the near future. Changing the way you approach upcoming events is crucial. Exposure without worry is the key. For example, you might use this self-coaching as a mantra in approaching whatever happens next:

"I can trust myself to deal with it when I get there."

As you are driving to work, you notice that you are going over the tasks that you will be faced with in the morning. You take a deep breath and, using a confident, positive and encouraging tone of voice, say to yourself:

"I can trust myself to deal with it when I get there. For now, I'll just let it go."

You might say it out loud, if appropriate, and then think it a few times as well. You emphasize the *can*. You do this a hundred times over the next three weeks, every time you notice the rumination beginning.

GUIDELINES FOR EXPOSURE THERAPY

- Do less than you are humanly capable of.
- Small steps are good.
- Pick goals that are meaningful to you.
- Be kind and compassionate with yourself.
- Persistence is the key.
- You have to repeatedly do something different if you want a different outcome.
- Repeated small steps will lead you out of the anxiety.
- Pick a task that's challenging but not overwhelming.
- Stack the deck in favour of your success.
- You can't win them all, but start winning some.
- You don't have to keep raising the bar.
- Keep doing the small steps until you're comfortable doing them.
- Raise the bar when you're bored with that step.
- Occasionally do too much or too little.
- Substitute: if you can't do the behavioural step that you planned, do another step. Continue to make progress.
- Stay in the situation until you feel your anxiety drop.
- If you have to leave, try not to go too far.
- Practice leaving the situation and then coming back.
- Practice the BC in the D.
- Identify your own covert avoidance.
- Surrender to being there.

MASTERING ANXIETY BY COMBINING BCD

Each of the volume dials has a powerful anxiety-decreasing effect. So why not use all three at once? Imagine yourself going into a situation that usually makes you anxious. This time, though, you have mastered breathing diaphragmatically, you are well practiced in coaching yourself using positive, encouraging self-talk and you have garnered the courage to fully engage in the situation while you are there.

You take a nice diaphragmatic breath and think:

"I can do this. I am going to do just fine," while using a confident and encouraging tone of voice. You briefly visualize yourself being relaxed and confident in the situation. Then, you enter the situation and fully participate in it, without holding back. You are turning all three volume dials way down simultaneously! Pow! Bam! Bfft! Take that, anxiety!

MASTERING ANXIETY THROUGH PROACTIVE LIVING

Now imagine living like that all the time and not just when you go into an anxiety-provoking situation. Mastering anxiety means that you make positive Breathing-Coaching-Doing your usual way of doing things; it's about learning to *live proactively* rather than reacting to events in your life. That means practice, practice, and practice. Practice when you're not anxious. If you were going into the final playoffs in basketball, you surely wouldn't wait until the game starts to begin practicing your skills. You would pick a place and time with no pressure and hone your skills until you felt comfortable and competent. Then, in the big game, your practiced skills would naturally emerge. You need to practice BCD in situations where you don't need them, so that in those situations where you do have anxiety, the skills kick in. Making BCD a part of your everyday life means that you are living proactively.

PART TWO

Finding Your Assertive Voice

11
The Nature of Assertiveness

"Be the change that you want to see in the world."

Mahatma Gandhi

JENNIFER'S TRANSFORMATION: PART I

Jennifer, a forty-two year-old, married woman, had been off work on stress leave. She started to feel better and managed to return to her workplace, but after several months at work she was alarmed to discover her old symptoms returning. She was once more feeling stressed, anxious, sad and overwhelmed. On Sunday night, she would ruminate about all the tasks waiting for her at work. She would try to plan out the next day's activities in her mind. She tossed and turned in bed and woke up several times during the night, her mind racing with worrying thoughts.

In the morning, she felt fatigued and drained from her restless sleep. She drove to work and as she approached the building where she worked, she noticed her heart start to race. Entering the elevator was the hardest part. She would stand in front of the elevator door, trying to summon the courage to press the button. On most mornings, she would simply be swept along by the crowd that was rushing to get a place in the elevator before it filled.

When she arrived on her floor, she was immediately confronted by a co-worker, who had many questions for her regarding her personal life. What had she done on her weekend? Why had she been off work for so long? Was she seeing a therapist? Was she taking anti-depressant medications? Which ones? How did she get along with her husband?

The co-worker would follow Jennifer around throughout the day and intrude into her physical workspace, determined to get an answer to her questions. Jennifer would crouch down at her desk, hang her head and look down at the floor. She began to hide in the washroom to get away from the co-worker. She found it hard to concentrate on her work and she became easily distracted from the task at hand. Jennifer always tried to do her absolute best at everything and she hated not being able to concentrate on her work. She felt like a failure.

After several months, she approached her manager about this workplace issue. She found the meeting exceedingly difficult, as she normally avoided conflict at all costs. It was only out of her increasing desperation that she finally mustered up the courage to speak with her manager. Hopefully, he would solve the issue and things could go then go back to normal.

Jennifer was shocked when her manager advised her that she should just tell the co-worker everything she wanted to know. Then, hopefully, the co-worker would be satisfied and stop asking more questions. The manager didn't like conflicts anymore than Jennifer did and he certainly wanted no part of this one.

Jennifer found it nearly impossible to stand up for her rights. Her inclination was to put others first, above herself. People-pleasing was important to her and she repeatedly sacrificed her own needs to meet the needs of others. She hoped that someone would then step up for her in return. Instead, she was regularly over-looked and taken for granted.

Jennifer felt powerless. She had difficulty being assertive. It felt like she had no voice in what happened to her and that she was simply swept along by outer events, like the crowd sweeping her into the elevator. Could learning to be assertive help Jennifer find her voice in this situation? What exactly is assertiveness?

ASSERTIVENESS DEFINED

Assertiveness can be defined as 'honest, clear and direct communication, that doesn't put the other person down.' There are two important elements in this definition. The first part of the definition – honest, clear and direct communication – discriminates assertiveness from passivity. In assertiveness you say what you honestly feel and think. You are real and authentic and your meaning is clear and evident. You don't hint or beat around the bush. You are specific rather than vague. The other person doesn't have to mind-read or guess what you are saying. Assertive communication is direct rather than indirect. That means you speak directly to the person involved, not to a third party about someone else.

The second part of the definition – doesn't put the other person down – discriminates assertiveness from aggression. You maintain a position of mutual respect with assertiveness. In contrast, when you are aggressive, you put the other person down by belittling or intimidating them. Assertiveness is always respectful as a communication, even when you are expressing anger or criticism. You are respectful of the other person and you respect yourself as well.

Practicing assertiveness results in empowerment in your relationships. You find your voice when you express, in an authentic and respectful way, what you genuinely think and feel. You become a presence in your relationships.

BASIC HUMAN RIGHTS

Assertiveness is based on the idea that all human beings have rights. You have rights and so does every other person. In assertiveness, you stand up for your rights while respecting those same rights in others. So, what are some of these basic human rights?

- The right to be treated with respect.
- The right to be treated in a way that reflects equality with others.
- The right to say no to things you don't want.
- The right to ask for what you do want.
- The right to be informed of decisions that are likely to affect you.
- The right to give and receive feedback in your relationships.
- The right to change your mind.
- The right to take your time to give an answer.

These represent some of the core basic human rights but the list is not meant to be exhaustive. What are some other rights that you consider important?

"You have a right to be here."

The Desiderata

THE VALUES OF ASSERTIVENESS

Assertiveness emerges from an underlying value system. These values include: authenticity; intimacy; equality; mutual respect; universal human rights; ownership; responsibility; accountability; and an optimism about human relationships. These core values provide direction and guidance to your assertive actions. If your behavior reflects these values, you are being assertive.

AUTHENTICITY

The great existentialist Jean-Paul Sartre described what he referred to as bad faith (Sartre, 1956), where one acts in such a way as to take on a role rather than being true to one's real self. Authenticity is the opposite of bad faith; to live authentically means you honor and respect your own opinions, beliefs and choices, in spite of the pressures to play certain social roles.

As noted earlier, William Shakespeare gave voice to this key existential thought four hundred years before Sartre. In Act 1 of Hamlet (1598), Polonius advises his son, as he prepares to leave home and go out into the world:
"This above all else: to thine own self be true."

Assertiveness fosters an awareness and expression of your true and authentic self. Conversely, the failure to live in a way that honors and respects your self is one of the causes of the pandemic of anxiety and depression in society. Patterns of self-sacrifice, exaggerated responsibility towards others, care-taking, avoidance of conflict at all costs and unrelenting perfectionism are recipes for anxiety and depression. If you are taught to ignore your own needs, to always look after others and strive for perfection in all things, you will most certainly have a great deal of anxiety as you try to live in such an unbalanced and unattainable way. You will lose touch with the sense of your *self*: your needs and what feels right to you. You become dis-empowered.

In order to live authentically, it is necessary to become aware of what you want in any given situation. You identify your own intentions so that you can attend to your internal authority. This means undertaking a path of self-knowledge. You develop an awareness of your own likes and dislikes as you take the time and effort to discover what feels right to you. You articulate your own values and beliefs and they guide your actions in the world, allowing you to live in a self-directed way.

To live authentically requires the skill of *tuning in* to your self. You cannot be 'true to thine self' if you don't first know your self. This is the key assertive question: What is it that you really want, think and feel? In assertiveness, tuning in to your self becomes a life-long endeavour; it's a way of being-in-the-world from moment to moment.

To live authentically also requires an act of courage. To be true to your self means that sometimes you must go against the socially acceptable response. It may well mean having a conflict with the next person. In living authentically, you develop comfortableness with conflict. Assertiveness gives you the tools for having a conflict in a way that is mutually respectful, authentic and non-escalating.

INTIMACY

Authenticity builds intimacy. You invite the other person in when you are genuine and open. This requires taking the time and effort to gain self-awareness so that you illuminate your own opinions, feelings and needs. Only then can others get to know you. In being assertive, you don't hide and so others come to know what you actually feel and what you truly like and don't like. When you choose to be authentic and transparent, you fully engage in deep, genuine and meaningful relationships with others.

EQUALITY, MUTUAL RESPECT AND
UNIVERSAL HUMAN RIGHTS

Assertiveness is based on equality, mutual respect and universal human rights. Everyone has the right to be treated with respect and everyone has a corresponding responsibility to treat others with respect, regardless of gender, age race, socio-economic status, sexual identity or any other affiliations. This applies to all people.

These are the core values of assertiveness: that all human beings have a right to be treated with respect, regardless of position or socially granted authority. I have the right to be treated with respect. So do you. Furthermore, everyone has that right equally: the homeless person has as much right to be treated with respect as the leader of the nation or the head of a corporation. It is true that some people have a profound impact on society while others may have only a small impact on a few individuals. The important thing is that everyone has a light to shine, no matter how big or small. That is what makes us all the same in terms of human rights. Everyone has the right to aspire to fulfill their potentials and to shine their light to the best of their abilities.

OWNERSHIP, RESPONSIBILITY AND ACCOUNTABILITY

Ownership, responsibility and accountability are vital aspects of the philosophy of assertiveness. You can't control what others do, but you can take charge of what you do; that's ownership. It is important to be proud of how you are handling situations in spite of what the other person does. How you handle the situation is your stuff and how they handle it is their stuff.

In assertiveness, ownership means that you take responsibility for your mistakes. We are all less than perfect, but we also strive to improve and learn as we go along. Making mistakes and being less than perfect are fundamental human traits. To err is not only human; it is inevitable. There is no good reason to deny those imperfections or to be ashamed of your shortcomings. However, there is very good reason to acknowledge your limitations as they emerge. That's precisely how you will grow and develop; that's how you learn. There is wisdom in acknowledging what you are doing well, while also recognizing what you can improve.

In assertiveness, you take responsibility for your own actions while holding others accountable for theirs. If someone is treating you in a way that is less than respectful, you let that person know. You give them feedback. You honor their right to know how they are doing in their relationship with you. Then, they can take responsibility for themselves and grow and develop based on your feedback.

OPTIMISM IN HUMAN RELATIONSHIPS

The philosophy of assertiveness manifests in a fundamentally positive world-view. Assertiveness is based on optimism regarding human relationships. The assumption is that others will rise to the occasion when and if given a chance to respond. If you are respectful, authentic and forthcoming with others, the anticipation is that they will behave in kind.

You work through conflicts by being upfront and honest with others. Conflicts tend to fester and escalate when not directly dealt with and adversarial positions become even more entrenched. When you choose optimism, you bring your issues to the person directly, give them the benefit of the doubt and allow them a chance to respond to your concerns. Whatever the outcome, you have respected the other person's right to know what is troubling you.

Of course there are always some who will not be respectful, even when approached assertively. Most people, though, will be glad to be given a chance to respond. Why sacrifice those relationships for the few people who are unable to be respectful back? Regardless of the outcome, what matters most is that you handle the situation in a way that you can be proud of, not how the other person responds.

EMPOWERMENT AND ASSERTIVENESS

Being assertive is an action; it's what you do. Empowerment is the experiential result of taking that assertive action. Empowerment can only come from you. No one else can give it to you. It's often easier and less anxiety provoking to do nothing, but inaction leaves you stuck and disempowered.

Taking action requires an act of courage. Empowerment results from finding the courage to express yourself in a genuine and open way.

Assertiveness is the behaviour of social empowerment. It is also the behaviour of self-esteem and of intimacy. All of those things require that you do something rather than remain passive. It is not enough simply to understand. You may grasp all the concepts in this book fully yet remain disempowered if you do not follow through and start to practice assertion. Nothing changes if you don't act.

Intimacy comes from getting to know someone and letting the other person get to know you. Assertive expression is your part of building that intimacy. It means that you tune in to yourself, identify your thoughts and emotions and then reveal what you are truly thinking and feeling in an open and honest way. Assertion is the act of expressing yourself and that is the act that creates intimacy.

Empowerment emerges from expressing truly what is in your heart. There is strength in the vulnerability of being open. That strength is in being authentic and true to yourself. Empowerment means you don't have to pretend or hide who you are. You don't try to be what you think that someone else wants you to be. You're true to yourself.

Self-esteem is a valuation of yourself that stems from your actions or inactions. Self-esteem develops from observing yourself as you deal with the challenges and activities in your life. If you are active in expressing yourself and in standing up for yourself, those judgements will be positive and therefore result in positive self-esteem. That will help you to develop confidence in yourself and to better cope with life in the future. You build self-assurance and self-esteem as you find your assertive voice.

12
Four Ways of
Being-in-the-World

*"Assertiveness takes the position of mutual respect
and equality."*

ASSERTIVENESS AS A WAY OF BEING-IN-THE-WORLD

Assertiveness is much more than a collection of skills; it is a way of being-in-the-world. It reflects the way you relate to others and the way you respect your *self*. Assertiveness can be viewed within the context of four possible styles of communication: passiveness, assertiveness, aggressiveness, and passive-aggressiveness. Each of these styles has it's own short and long term consequences, goals, interpersonal position, relative effectiveness, response from others and underlying etiology. Each of these ways of being-in-the-world can also be seen as holding a certain position on rights, regarding your own rights and the rights of others.

You are likely to engage in each of these communication patterns at times, but problems arise when one of the more negative modes becomes a habitual style of interaction. If you are usually passive, aggressive or passive-aggressive, you will inevitably experience problems with self-worth, difficulties in interpersonal relationships and ongoing feelings of powerlessness and frustration. Conversely, if you are generally assertive about what is important to you, then you will reap significant benefits in confidence and in building positive relationships.

Assertiveness is the behavior of empowerment, intimacy and self-esteem. You take your place at the table as you find and express your assertive voice. Assertiveness builds empowerment and mitigates depression and anxiety.

In learning assertiveness, the first step is to recognize these four ways of being-in-the-world.

THE ONE-DOWN POSITION

Taking a one-down position in your relationships means that you give up your rights while allowing others to have rights. You are one-down while they are one-up. Passiveness is about *not doing*: it means not standing up for your rights; not asking for what you want; or saying yes when you really mean no. You let things happen to you and around you that you don't really want. It means that you don't have a voice.

TAKING A ONE-DOWN POSITION IS PASSIVE

Passiveness is a submissive position. It is one-sided, with the focus being on the other person; you give respect to the other person, but not to yourself. The other person is elevated while you assume a lowered position in the relationship:

"You have rights but I don't."

"It's important that you are happy, but I don't matter."

"I'll go along with whatever you want."

Taking a one-down position is like being a child in an

adult world. You are smaller and have fewer rights than the big people. This can be visibly demonstrated in your posture: bowing down, head hung low and eyes downcast. It is as though you don't really deserve to take up all that room so you are trying to cram yourself into a much smaller space. Your shoulders slump and your entire demeanor takes a downward and inward stance. You may even start to feel smaller or younger than others when you take this one-down posture, as your physical posture shifts your state of mind.

This self-effacing posture sends a powerful message to others and to yourself. It says that you are somehow *less* than others. In poker, downward movements are often a 'tell' for a weak hand; your posture unconsciously communicates to others that you don't deserve respect.

PASSIVENESS IS INDIRECT AND CAN BE DISHONEST

As a form of communication, passiveness is indirect. What you are genuinely feeling is only hinted at, rather than being clearly articulated:

"There's sure a lot of dishes on the counter."

"Oh, you're going to be late again?"

"It must be nice to just take the day for yourself."

You hint that you would like someone to wash the dishes and clean the counter. You are not happy that the other person is going to be late because that upsets the plans that you have made. You actually don't want the other person to take the day off because you have planned to get some work done and you would like a little help. However, none of this is stated clearly. Instead, it is hinted at and so it is now up to the other person to read between the lines in order to figure out what you mean. Indirect communication can be manipulative, like a guilt-trip.

Passiveness can be dishonest by omission. When you don't say what you really want, the implication is that you are happy with the present state of affairs, when that is not actually the case.

If you are afraid to upset anyone, you find it hard to express any position that might be offensive or contrary. This can result in dishonest communication:

"We will be glad to have you and your family stay with us for two weeks."

"I don't mind working late again."

"I'm really sorry I don't have any spare change to give you."

If the statements above do not reflect your true feelings, they are dishonest. You are not really glad to have a house full of guests for two weeks. You don't want to work late tonight and you didn't want to the last time either, even though you did. An apology is dishonest if it is not authentic. Perhaps you are not actually sorry about not having spare change. Maybe you even have change in your pocket right now, but you are choosing not to give it out.

PASSIVENESS, OWNERSHIP AND ACCOUNTABILITY

Passiveness means that you avoid taking ownership for yourself and what you want. Instead, you give in to the wishes of others; you go along with others while ignoring your own needs. As a result, you might be filled with resentment and anger about how others are treating you. Your part in that treatment, though, is that you don't stand up for yourself; you don't say what it is that you don't like. Ownership means that you would take the time to identify how you feel and then give voice to that. In passiveness, you might not even know what it is that you don't like. You lose your voice.

Passiveness also means that you don't hold others accountable for their actions. Passiveness is at the root of many social problems such as unquestioning obedience to authority and tolerating harassment or bullying. Problems like bullying continue when you look the other way instead of holding the bully accountable for their actions. Passiveness enables disrespectful behavior and leads to a loss of your inner direction as you look to others for how you should behave.

THE ORIGINS OF PASSIVENESS

There are a number of pathways that can lead to a passiveness. Fear of conflict is a prime motivation for interpersonal deference. That anxiety can emerge from a history of trying to cope with a threatening world. For example, if you experienced childhood verbal, physical or sexual abuse, you quickly learned that it was dangerous to stand up for yourself. You became more concerned with your safety than with your rights. You learned to keenly observe others and then placate them, before things got out of hand. Indirect manipulation became your usual way of interacting with others, not from a sense of power and control, but rather from a place of fear and insecurity. Passiveness can be driven by efforts to achieve safety, but you pay the price of losing your voice. You become dis-empowered.

Passiveness can be driven by an emotional neediness that manifests in people-pleasing. If you didn't receive enough care and approval in your developing years, you remain thirsty for affection. You try to make others happy in order to gain the missing affection. You put your own needs on the back burner in an effort to appease others. You secretly hope that the other person will finally love and appreciate you in return. You seek other-esteem in order to attain self-esteem:

"If I make everyone happy, they will be so pleased with me that they will return the favor and then I will finally get my needs met."

Unfortunately, that bargain is rarely fulfilled and you end up overlooked instead. You feel your self slipping away in unmet needs and unspoken words.

Another pathway to passivity is through patterns of self-sacrifice that are taught as positive social values. The word 'selfish' has a clearly negative tone, yet there is no equivalent derogatory word for over-doing for others; "self-lessness" carries only a positive connotation. It is held up as a value and model to be emulated. Selfishness, on the other hand is clearly not portrayed as having any positive attribute:

"Don't blow your own horn," and:

"Make sure you share," but rarely do we hear:

"Make sure you get what you need, too."

The message is that you are a good person when you look after others, but there is no corresponding view that you are a good person if you look after yourself. Females, in particular, are taught that they should 'always be nice' to others. This is another way of saying: be passive, please other people and overlook your own needs. These social values are pervasively transmitted through the media and through modeling.

Children who witness these patterns of self-sacrifice in their parents emulate them in order to gain love and approval. Imitating the behaviors that they see around them, they become the next generation of self-sacrificing care-takers, in an effort to internalize a sense of being worthwhile and lovable.

SHORT AND LONG TERM CONSEQUENCES OF PASSIVENESS

What are some of the short and long term consequences to being passive? One immediate consequence is that your level of anxiety goes down. If you don't stand up for your self, the other person will therefore not be angry and so the conflict gets avoided. The drop in anxiety is highly reinforcing:

"Whew, I avoided that and now everybody's happy."

"I gave in, so now there's no argument."

If you give in, go along and don't rock the boat, the potential threat is avoided and you breathe a sigh of relief. You are safe. It means that you will be passive in the future, because safety is a primal and powerful motivation.

In the longer term, passiveness has many negative consequences. It keeps you in the one-down position. It manifests in low self-esteem as your sense of self is diminished. You become like a child in an adult world; you feel helpless, powerless and smaller compared to others. You look for opportunities to placate or manipulate others in an attempt to be safe and prevent potential bad things from happening. You become a chameleon, trying to fit in by being what you guess that others think you should be. You are not sure who you really are anymore. You lose your unique voice. When you are passive, you become out of touch with yourself, with what you want and how you feel.

You observe yourself constantly pleasing others and then form a negative judgment about yourself. That reinforces your low self-esteem, leads to more frantic efforts to please others and results in a style of self-critical style of thinking:

"Why didn't I say anything?"

"I must be a wimp, I'm letting them walk all over me."

"I should be handling this better."

This self-berating style of thinking only reinforces your low self-esteem and results in feelings of worthlessness.

Another significant, long-term consequence to a passive style of living is that you build negative relationships with others. If you are frequently giving in to the wishes of others, you train those around you to not consider your feelings. The implication is that you must be happy with the way things are going, because of your lack of complaint. Passivity sends the message:

"Everything is just fine with me, I like the way things are going."

Some people may repeatedly ask you what you want, but eventually give up when no clear response is forthcoming. You get taken for granted in your relationships and you end up agreeing to things you don't want. You find yourself babysitting a family of four kids over the weekend or having a disliked acquaintance move in to your apartment for three months when you continually say yes to things that you don't actually want. This may be a re-creation of a childhood experience where you were treated as though you were not important and that your needs didn't matter. The resulting core belief – I don't matter – gets reinforced in adult experiences as you repeatedly take a one-down position in your relationships.

Friends and family members may experience a sense of frustration and helplessness in the face of your continued passive behaviors. If you rarely declare what you want from others, it becomes impossible for them to help you out. Especially in close relationships, it is important that the people who care about you feel that they can do things to make you happy. This generates a sense of interpersonal competence and fosters closeness in your relationships. Passiveness frustrates your friends and family.

When you are passive, you swallow your resentments and disappointments. These can build up over time, in a volcanic fashion. Each new slight is added to the underlying well of frustrations and anger. Eventually the resentments may spill over, in a venting and aggressive manner that is far out of proportion to the incident. You say things you wish you could take back. You belittle the other person because you are so charged with adrenalin. Then, seeing the damage that has just taken place, you vow to never again say what you think. You flip-flop between periods of passiveness and intermittent episodes of aggression.

THE ONE-UP POSITION

Taking a One-Up Position is Aggressive

Aggressiveness means that you put the other person down. Aggression is one-sided, with the focus being on you. You respect what you want but you disrespect the other person. In aggression you take a one-up position in your relationship:

"I have rights, but you don't."

"I have more rights than you."

"I am more important than you."

"You will shut up and listen to me."

Aggression belittles, puts down, dominates or intimidates the other person. This disrespect can take the form of insults; using a loud tone of voice; uttering threats; being condescending; standing in someone's personal space; towering over a seated person; or simply pointing a finger.

Physically, you take a one-up position. The posture of aggression is to be above, looming over or talking down to the other person. In aggression, you put the other person down. You crowd into their physical space. You raise your hand, your voice and your posture and take the position of being above the other person.

Aggression represents an escalation of a conflict. You take the interaction up a notch. Then the other person has two choices: either give in and take a passive position, or further escalate the situation in an attempt to recover from the one-down position. You go one-up and they go one further up.

Aggression Can Be Honest and Direct

Aggression tends to be direct rather than the indirect, as seen in passiveness. You might blast the person directly, as you literally get up into their face. Aggression involves conflict and confrontation, but does so in a one-sided, escalating and disrespectful way. It intimidates and demeans the other person.

Sometimes there is honesty in aggression. Remember the adage:

"Many a truth gets spoken in anger."

However, in aggression you are not looking for an open and honest dialogue, but rather to vent and impose your will on the other person. Aggressive communication is one-sided with the focus being on the aggressor. You are going to have your say and they are going to listen. You will be brutally honest, but you are not willing to listen in return. The honesty in aggression does not foster intimacy, but instead promotes fear, distance and anger. You are honest but not respectful. The message is:

"You're going to listen to me whether you like it or not."
"I will tell you."
"I'm right and you're wrong."
"I'm smart and you're stupid."

Aggression, Ownership and Accountability

In aggression you do hold others accountable for their behavior, but you do it in a disrespectful way. You tell them exactly what you think of what they did, but you blast them and put them down when you do.

In aggression, you accuse the other person, so your statements often start with "You..." rather than "I..." The result is that while you hold others accountable, you blame them for how you feel rather than taking ownership for your own thoughts and feelings. Instead, your anger is dumped onto the other person.

The Origins of Aggressiveness

Aggression is driven by the emotions of anger, powerlessness and fear. If you have been chronically passive, you can still erupt into aggression once you have collected enough resentment to override your feelings of powerlessness and apprehension.

Aggression often comes from a place of powerlessness. Your behavior is inflated because you feel so small; you talk loud because you don't feel heard. Deep-seated feelings of ineffectiveness manifest in angry outbursts in an attempt to regain a sense of empowerment:

"If I yell at you, then you will finally hear me."

Aggressive people are often stunned when I suggest that they need assertiveness training:

"My wife thinks I am way too assertive already, doc!"

If you tend towards aggression as a style, you probably lack a true sense of empowerment. Instead, you might have a sense of inadequacy and a corresponding anger at the world. You may have been ignored, abused and victimized by others in the past. You have been hurt and now you want to lash out; you put others down because you expect them to put you down. You feel powerless and insignificant and you vent your anger in an effort to regain a sense of personal power that is lacking.

Fear is another motivation for aggression. You may assume a menacing and threatening demeanor as a way to try to protect yourself. You have decided that the best defense is a good offense. Others see you as visibly threatening and then give you a wide berth. Your physical presence says:

"Don't come near me!"

On the outside you appear dangerous and menacing but on the inside you are terrified. You feel threatened and so you scare other people away before they even think about approaching you. Your aggressive appearance is an attempt to make yourself safe in a threatening world.

Short and Long-Term Consequences of Aggressiveness

What are the consequences of aggression? One result can be a feeling of power:

"At least I didn't let them push me around! I told them!"

You gave voice to what you honestly thought. You stood up for yourself and in the immediate moment that felt good. You expressed the voice that you don't usually have. You went from powerless to powerful.

The long-term consequences of aggression are, however, the same as those of the passive style: low self-esteem, powerlessness and negative interpersonal relationships.

You feel shame as you realize the disrespectful nature of your aggressive expression. Yes, you spoke your truth, but you really put the other person down and you don't feel proud of the way you behaved. Your aggression was out of proportion to the actual issue at hand. You demeaned the other person. You feel embarrassed by how you handled the situation and you vow to bottle things up in the future.

Others walk on eggshells around you, never being certain as to what might set you off. Will you be passive or will you explode? Other aggressive people may seek you out in a 'toughest gunslinger' fashion. Others may deliberately push your buttons as a way of retaliating for feeling belittled by your outbursts in the past.

People now approach you with the expectation that you will put them down. They watch you for signs of arrogance and condescension and interpret your actions through that filter. Your relationships become filled with conflict and you find that you can trust no one. You have to constantly watch your back.

Both the aggressive and passive styles result in feelings of dis-empowerment, low self-esteem and negative relationships with others. You know that you are not handling things very well, but you are unsure as to what to do about it.

In order to overcome the aggressive style, it is important that you develop a true sense of empowerment. You need to claim your voice, but also to make it a respectful one that you can be proud of later.

A Different Type of Aggression: The Sociopath

Some aggressive behavior has an aspect of cruelty from which the aggressor derives satisfaction. For sociopaths, part of their pre-frontal cortex is turned off so that they are unable to experience empathy for the pain of others. As a result, the sociopath can obtain pleasure from controlling and manipulating others with no shame or guilt arising from their aggression. Sociopaths lack empathy for others and are missing a sense of remorse over their own behavior. When dealing with an aggressive person, it is important to discriminate between these two very different types of aggressive people.

THE ONE-BEHIND POSITION

Whereas passiveness involves taking a one-down position and aggression a one-up position, passive-aggression takes a one-behind position. You attack the other person from behind. You shoot your arrows while you remain hidden in the bushes. You both hide and attack: that's the passive and the aggressive elements.

Taking a One-Behind Position is Passive-Aggressive

Passive-aggressiveness results from a blending of two styles: passiveness and aggression. Passive-aggression can be described as hidden hostility. It punishes, which is aggressive, but does so in an indirect way, so it is also passive.

If you are the recipient of passive-aggressive behavior, you feel like you have been stabbed in the back, but you can't be entirely sure. When you are passive-aggressive, you behave quite differently to someone's face than when they are out of earshot. You smile in their face but scowl at their back.

One of the most common forms of passive-aggression is the cold shoulder.

For example, you notice that your spouse is slamming the cupboard doors and rattling the dishes:

"What's the matter, sweetie – is something bothering you?"

"No, I'm fine."

"Are you sure? You seem upset about something?"

"NO, I SAID I'M FINE!!"

Hopefully, this doesn't last for long and then the two of you can discuss what the problem is and work your way through it. For some people though, passive-aggression becomes a style of communicating and so the cold shoulder can continue for weeks or even months. This is incredibly destructive to the relationship. Animosity becomes entrenched. Resentments seethe and simmer. Walls get built that are difficult to dismantle. Intimacy is lost, replaced with the cold chill of disapproval. You withdraw into yourself in defense against the feelings of rejection. It's a hard place to come back from. To make matters worse, you may not even know what the issues are because communication has been switched off.

Passive-Aggression is Hidden, Indirect,
Dishonest and Sabotaging

Some other examples of passive-aggression are: being late for a meeting, neglecting to pass on important information, engaging in sarcasm, feigning friendship, damaging someone's property, creating scenarios that cause problems for someone or being critical behind someone's back while praising them to their face.

How do you know when someone is being passive-aggressive? We've all been late for a meeting and we're pretty sure that the intent wasn't to punish anyone. This is one of the difficulties of passive-aggression: the intention is hidden and has to be inferred. That leaves plenty of room for doubt and confusion about what is being expressed. Is something going on here or are you imagining things?

Passive-Aggression Denies Ownership

When you are passive-aggressive, you avoid ownership by denying any malicious intent when confronted:

"It feels like you are sabotaging me by not telling me about this meeting."

"Oh, you're way too sensitive. I just forgot." (This said with a pleasant smile.)

The above (real) example illustrates a master of passive-aggression as the put-downs continue (you're too sensitive) as you confront the behavior in an attempt to bring it out into the open. This makes passive-aggressive behavior the most difficult style to deal with of the four ways of being-in-the-world. Aggression tends to be direct and clear as a communication. You know where you stand and what the issues are, making it possible to resolve them. Passive-aggression, on the other hand, hides the issues – even denies that there are issues – making resolution unlikely.

Passive-aggressiveness comes dressed in plausible deniability. In passive-aggressiveness, you have the luxury of hiding out in the indirectness of the communication, while taking pot shots from the bushes. Herein lies the *raison d'être* for passive-aggressive behavior. Remember that passiveness is motivated by fear while aggression is motivated by anger. Passive-aggression allows you to hide out (fear based behavior), while attacking from the bushes (anger based behavior.)

The Origins of Passive-Aggressiveness

Why would you engage in passive-aggression when it is such an ineffective and self-destructive form of communication? If you are passive-aggressive as a *style* – not just the occasional cold shoulder – you likely grew up in an environment that fostered both fear and anger. There was generally good reason to be angry about something, but also very good reason to be afraid of expressing that anger. This sets up a dilemma; you are furious about how you are being treated but you know you will get severely punished if you say anything. Passive-aggression is the unhappy solution to this dilemma. You learn to express anger while pretending not to. For example, one sibling unfairly blames another for breaking something, then smiles as their sibling takes the punishment meant for them. They manipulate the aggressor while setting up their sibling to take the fall. Someone else gets punished and they avoid any repercussions.

Another example of passive-aggression is playing the role of the martyr as a way of guilt-tripping others. You are the noble and long-suffering hero in the face of unjust treatment. The intent is to indirectly shame the other person. You are the innocent and injured party while the other person is clearly the bad one:

"I know you're too busy to drive me even though my back hurts. You just go on with your day, I'll be alright."

If you give in, you will do so with resentment because you know you have been manipulated. If you don't give in, you feel guilty, but either way you lose.

These behaviors often appear puzzling and unfathomable to others. That's because the passive-aggressive person is re-enacting historical patterns from their past. These actions may make absolutely no sense whatsoever in the present day context because they are more about how the person was treated as a child. Passive-aggressiveness is a re-enactment of childhood experiences. But, in childhood, an outside observer could understand the passive-aggressive behaviors in the context of what was happening in the home. When these child behavioral patterns time-travel into the present-day home and office, colleagues and family are left bewildered and resentful. The passive-aggressive actions appear mysterious and inexplicable. Others may respond with anger, anxiety and mistrust:

"Watch your back with this one!"

It usually isn't long before others begin to respond with passive-aggression in kind, to retaliate against these inexplicable attacks. A battle has been unwittingly commenced, but the rules of engagement are unclear. The only thing you can know for sure is that more punishment is coming.

Short and Long-Term Consequences of Passive-Aggressiveness

A short-term consequence of passive-aggression is a brief sense of power over others. You sow confusion and discord all around you and then you stand back and watch the fun. This sense of satisfaction, however, can be quite fleeting, as others retaliate or withdraw, living you isolated and with few friends or allies. Passive-aggression has the long–term effects of alienation from others, self-perpetuation of negative childhood relationship patterns, low self-esteem, and ongoing anxiety in the social world. You are not really living in the present. Instead, you are re-creating a world in which there is little safety. The only bit of safety you can find is to hide in the chaos that you create.

A passive-aggressive style manifests in paranoia and hyper-vigilance to the social world, as you continuously scan for signs of threat. These attacks do indeed appear, as the anger and mistrust of others results in retaliation, thus confirming your sense of the world as a dangerous place.

Passive-aggressiveness is exceedingly self-defeating. It is the least effective way of being-in-the-world and also the most difficult one to respond to in an effective way. The style of passive-aggression manifests in ongoing self-destructive patterns, chaotic relationships and a chronic unhappiness with life.

THE POSITION OF MUTUAL RESPECT
AND EQUALITY OF RIGHTS

Taking a Position of Mutual Respect and Equality is Assertive

In passiveness you are one-down, in aggression you go one-up and in passive-aggression you take a one-behind position. With assertiveness, you take a position of mutual respect and equality:

"I have rights and so do you."

"We both deserve to be treated with respect."

"You have the right to ask me for something and I have the right to say no."

Assertiveness is about having an equal and mutually respectful relationship. When you are assertive you take the position:

"I will respect you, but I will also respect myself and my rights as well. I will call you to account if you don't respect me."

Assertiveness takes a face-to-face, equal stance. It's about taking responsibility for your self, while still respecting others. In assertiveness, you assume the position of an adult in an adult world.

If you take some time to think about the people in your life who are consistently assertive, what impression do you have of them? Would you want them for a friend? A boss? A colleague? For many people the answer is a resounding yes. In fact, the assertive people are often seen as role models:

"I wish I could be more like them."

If an assertive person asks you for something, it is clear and direct and so you don't feel manipulated or confused by their request. You know where you stand because they tell you how they feel. It's genuine. They don't insult or disrespect others and you don't have to guess or mind-read to know what they're thinking; you just ask. You go to the assertive person when you truly want an honest answer.

Furthermore, it feels *safe* to talk with someone who is assertive, because they treat you with respect; there are no put-downs, sarcasm or gossip behind your back. Safety enhances trust and intimacy in a relationship and you can be yourself in the relationship. It's easier for you to be authentic when you are in a relationship with someone who is assertive.

Assertive people are also viewed as more confident in themselves. Confidence is one of the factors associated with sexual desirability and appeal, so it's not a stretch to say that assertiveness can make you sexy. Save money and hold off on the new wardrobe and plastic surgery; just start being more assertive.

Assertiveness is Honest, Clear and Direct

The definition of assertiveness is: *honest, clear and direct communication that does not put the other person down*. In assertiveness, you are honest in expressing yourself and you are clear and specific in the communication, rather than vague or general. Furthermore, the communication is expressed directly to the person involved. You don't go behind the other person's back. These elements distinguish assertiveness from passiveness.

Assertiveness is Respectful

The second part of the definition of assertion: *'that does not put the other person down,'* distinguishes assertiveness from aggression. You stand your ground, but you do so without bullying, intimidating or threatening the other person. In assertion, you maintain a position of respectfulness throughout your interaction. You neither escalate into aggression, nor do you back down and disrespect yourself.

Assertiveness, Ownership and Accountability

You can't control how others react to you, but you can control how you act. Being assertive means that you take ownership for your actions. You assume responsibility for the things that concern you and for how you interact with others. If you are unhappy with how someone is treating you, you go and talk to them directly. You hold them accountable for their actions and you do that in a respectful way.

You remain assertive throughout the interaction, regardless of the actions of the other. You act rather than react. Proactivity is a central aspect of both assertiveness and empowerment.

The Origins of Assertiveness

Assertiveness naturally emerges from positive beliefs about your self; that you have rights and that you deserve to be treated with respect. It's based on the understanding that you *do* matter and that you have equal importance to others. Assertiveness requires an act of courage but results in confidence and self-esteem, which then leads to feelings of personal empowerment. You find your voice when you choose to be assertive.

One of the pathways to assertiveness is through having a care-giver that fostered assertiveness in you. In your childhood, someone tuned in to you on a regular basis and reflected what you were thinking and feeling. It was clear that you mattered. That person offered you choices and making those choices helped you to find out what you liked and what you didn't like. Eventually, you internalized this respect for yourself.

You developed the ability to tune into your self and to identify what you were thinking and feeling. You became self-aware. It felt safe enough for you to express yourself without fear. If you said no to something, your care-giver listened and tried to understand what you were feeling and what you wanted. They also modeled assertive behavior, so that you had an example to follow. They expressed what they liked and set limits with things they didn't want. They did this in a respectful but firm way. You watched and learned.

Perhaps you didn't have the nurturing experience of an assertive care-giver. The good news is that you can learn to be assertive and you are already on your way there by working on the skills in this book. Finding your assertive voice will help you overcome negative patterns that keep you anxious, powerless and mired in low self-esteem.

Short and Long-Term Consequences of Assertiveness

In the short term, assertiveness can result in an increase in anxiety as you face the situation head on. Anxiety is there to help you avoid situations that are seen as threatening. When you go into a difficult situation, your anxiety increases to alert you to the danger and to help you to leave. Assertiveness takes an act of courage because it challenges that very human desire to avoid those unpleasant things that involve conflict.

Confronting the situation can result in an increase in your anxiety, but, as you stay in the situation, your anxiety begins to drop. You learn that it's not so bad after all. You learn that you can actually bring things out into the open and work through them. In confronting the situation, you get to know where the other person stands and they get to know where you stand. This clarifies any misperceptions that were present. You get at the facts rather than the interpretations. You gain a sense of the reality of the situation.

Assertiveness becomes more comfortable with practice and experience. The long-term consequences of living assertively over time can be truly life transforming. You become comfortable in expressing yourself and in dealing with conflict. The most significant long-term consequences of assertion are personal empowerment, self-esteem and positive interpersonal relationships. Notice that *getting what you want* wasn't on that list, although assertiveness is generally the most effective and respectful method for achieving that goal. However, the latter goal pales in importance to the extraordinarily important consequences of developing a sense of empowerment, building self-esteem and fostering positive relationships. It is less important to go away from a situation saying:

"Good, I got what I wanted," than it is to say:

"I stood up for myself and I liked the way I handled that."

When you do get what you want, you can feel good about the way you went about it.

Another long-term consequence of assertiveness is that you learn to live authentically, in a way that respects your self, but also lets other people in. You allow people to get to know you when you tune in to yourself and express what you truly feel and think. This deepens the intimacy in your relationships; your connection to others becomes more vibrant and meaningful. You gain a voice and you take your place at the table in your relationships.

You become less susceptible to the influence of others when you are assertive. You are less likely to go along with things that you feel are wrong or questionable. You resist peer pressure. Instead, you develop obedience to yourself as you learn to acknowledge and respect your own ethical and moral codes. You develop a feeling of solidity within yourself as you live your life based on your internal compass rather than in response to the weather of the day.

Self-esteem is another important consequence of assertiveness. You can't control how others respond to your assertion, but how you handle the situation determines whether you feel proud or ashamed. You observe yourself dealing with things and then you consider how you did in that situation. If you were assertive, you will feel good about yourself, regardless of the outcome. That's self-esteem; you develop a sense of mastery in approaching things. Self-efficacy is the belief that you can manage things and that belief is learned through assertiveness. Self-efficacy manifests in confidence and the willingness to take on new things, as you trust yourself to be able to deal with the challenges that arise. It means you believe in yourself.

13
Elements of an Assertive Voice

"What do you want?"

LEARNING TO LIVE ASSERTIVELY

How do you learn to live in an assertive way? Fortunately, there are a number of core assertive skills that are straightforward, easy to learn and will help find your assertive voice. Mastering these skills will result in enhanced empowerment in your relationships. These are the skills of social empowerment. It would be a very different world if these core skills were taught to all students as respectful and resilient ways of being with each other.

Assertiveness results in deepened connections with others, enhanced self-esteem and reduced anxiety. In practicing assertiveness, you develop confidence in yourself as you realize that you can manage the challenges that you face in the world.

Assertiveness requires an act of courage on your part. There may have been events in your past that have kept you in a submissive role. Your past may have fostered fear, anxiety and avoidance. In order to overcome those obstacles, you will need to tolerate some anxiety as you try out new behaviors in the present. You come out into the open when your instincts are telling you to hide. Assertiveness starts with an act of faith, in spite of your fear: it's an act of faith in your self.

It will be necessary to identify and overcome any internal obstacles to assertiveness. Those cognitive barriers are negative core beliefs, which are internalizations of self-limiting patterns such as: people pleasing; self–sacrifice; exaggerated duty to others; perfectionism; obedience to authority; and avoidance of conflict at all costs.

ELEMENTS OF AN ASSERTIVE VOICE:

- Identify What You Want in the Situation
- Be Specific and Clear
- Start Your Assertion with "I"
- Don't Soften the Blow
- Only Bring Up One Issue at a Time
- Sort the Issues
- Congruence Between the Verbal and the Non-verbal Communication
- The Power of Maintaining an Assertive Stance
- The Right Time and Place

IDENTIFY WHAT YOU WANT IN THE SITUATION

Assertiveness starts by posing the question:

"What do I want in this situation?"

Answering that question, in a clear and specific way, can be more difficult than it sounds. It requires tuning in to your self in order to determine what you really want or don't want. The art of tuning in to your self is the fundamental skill of assertiveness; it is the starting point for all assertive behaviour. Over time, with repeated practice, the self-knowledge becomes much more accessible and spontaneous.

"I want you to treat me with respect. By that I mean that I want you to be on time for our meetings."

"I don't want to go out tonight. I would like to just stay in and relax."

"I want you to fill up the car with gas when you use it."

It may take some time and thought to clearly answer the question:

"What do I want in this situation?"

If you are not sure of what you want, stop and give yourself time to reflect. Many communications go badly because of the failure to fully complete step one. It is difficult, if not impossible, to be assertive when you don't really know what it is that you want. Being clear about what you want is the foundation of assertiveness.

Eventually, this process of self-knowledge becomes more spontaneous as tuning in to your self becomes your customary way of being-in-the-world. The good news is that, if you didn't learn this skill as a child, it's not too late to learn it now.

Identifying what you want means that you take ownership for those needs. You have the right to want things from others, but it is *you* who are ultimately responsible for asserting that right.

Be wary of the *should*s:

"He should know better than that."

"She should be more respectful."

"They shouldn't treat me like that."

It is easy to become side-tracked on what the other person might be doing wrong, rather than what it is that you want in the situation. Then you fall into reacting to the other person's actions rather than proactively putting forth your position. The more you rail against the other person and paint them as the bad guy in the picture, the more emotionally reactive you become. Your negative view can easily become exaggerated and distorted with criticisms, interpretations and indignation.

Mentally ranting against the other person doesn't give the other person the benefit of the doubt or offer them the chance to respond to your concerns. It also takes the focus off of identifying what it is that you want. If you find that you are getting caught up in judging the other person, bring your focus back to what it is that you want in the situation. Ownership and responsibility naturally follow from that process. The situation becomes less emotional and it is easier to be active rather than reactive when you are not charged up with adrenalin and anger. Have your emotions inform your actions rather than direct them.

Stick with what you want *in that particular situation*, rather than trying for a more general change in behavior. The general issues tend to take care of themselves when you address the specific issues that arise. For example, if you want someone to treat you with more respect, be clear as to what that means in the specific situation. In the example above, respect meant being on time for the meeting.

Sometimes you might want more than one thing. Then you have to decide what is the most important to you. What is it that you really want the most?

A mother would drive her son to his baseball games and practices, often in rush hour traffic, which, under any other circumstances, she would do her best to avoid. The schedule of the baseball activities unfortunately necessitated frequent rush hour drives, and these drives resulted in ongoing feelings of irritation and frustration for the mother/chauffer. On pondering what she wanted in this situation, though, the mother came to an unexpected conclusion and developed some surprising insights into her relationship with her son. Her son would typically utter only monosyllabic grunts in response to queries as to how his day had gone. However, he would actually talk at great length and with some passion about the concerns of his life, when they were riding together in the car. It occurred to her that this might be because they were seated side-by-side, rather than face-to-face and that she was attending to the driving and not so fully focused on him. It seemed that these factors made it much easier for her teenage son to talk and open up – probably the thinking behind the architectural design of the confession booth.

The mother realized that what she truly wanted was to be able to converse with her son in this open and unguarded way. She missed that. Regaining those moments of connection became her priority while enduring the heavy traffic paled in importance. Her irritation evaporated and she began to actually enjoy her chauffering duties. She became adept in appearing not to be focused on him. She mastered the art of giving her son space to talk without appearing to be questioning him. She got to know her son all over again in spite of him becoming a teenager who had become incommunicado.

BE SPECIFIC AND CLEAR

It is helpful to make the answer to the question: 'What do you want in this situation?' as specific as you can. Sometimes your first answers are vague or general:

"I want him to be more considerate."

"I want them to show some respect."

How? By doing what exactly? Describe precisely what you would like with enough detail so the answer is clear to all concerned.

You can't be assertive if you don't know what you want. The answer needs to be so clear that, *if the other person were to agree with you, the solution to the problem would be obvious.* Specificity and clarity are fundamental qualities of assertive communication.

"I want you to be more considerate," is not clear and therefore the solution to the problem is not obvious.

"I want you to be on time when we have a meeting scheduled," has much greater clarity. The solution is obvious if the person were to agree; if the meeting is set for noon, show up no later than noon.

Other examples of vagueness:

"I want them (children) to treat me with more respect."

"I want him (husband) to help out more. He *never* does anything!"

Now, these are certainly reasonable things to want, but they lack specificity. So be specific: what is the husband to do that would result in the wife feeling respected or helped? The answer in the above example is not clear. Even if the husband were to agree that her request is valid and that he is willing to go along with her request he may not know what is expected of him. So the question then becomes:

"What, specifically, can your husband do to ensure that you will feel that you are being helped?"

Maybe your answer is:

"Well, he *should* know that without me saying."

Articulating your request in a clear, honest and direct way, honors the other person's right to know what it is that you want from them. It's mutually respectful communication; it respects both yourself and the other person. Clear and honest communication reflects optimism in your relationships with others:

"If I clearly tell him what it is that I want, he will gladly help me."

You give him the benefit of the doubt and now it is at least possible for him to rise to the occasion. He might be more than happy to be able to help out. He might even feel a huge sense of relief in finally knowing what will make you happy. It's a powerful feeling to be able to have such an impact on someone you love; it's the feeling of competence.

For example, one woman narrowed down her answer from:

"He *shouldn't* be so lazy and selfish," to:

"I want him to do the dishes three times a week."

She was then able to make the request in a very assertive way directly to her husband. His response was not at all what she had expected. He was happy that he could do something to help her and have some impact on her moods – alternating between anger and depression – to which he had felt entirely helpless to respond. He helped most days with the dishes, as requested, but also, on his own initiative, he began to cook half of the meals. He went to a cooking class and started to explore gourmet cooking, discovering a hidden (and vastly appreciated) talent. Their relationship improved dramatically and they began to do things together in preparation of retirement.

She became less depressed and more active in her community. She was able to generalize the skill of making requests to others beyond her spouse, to her great benefit. She emerged from chronic feelings of helplessness, frustration and powerlessness and experienced a burgeoning feeling of empowerment. She became aware of the impact she had on those around her. This sent her on a completely different trajectory than the previous, decades old, pattern of passivity, helplessness and resentment.

If you have anxiety, you are probably thinking:

"OK, but what if..."

What if you are clear and specific and yet the other person still doesn't respect your wishes? You repeatedly and clearly state what you want but the other person adamantly refuses to respect your wishes. That tells you something very important; your assertiveness has illuminated an underlying lack of respect. That illumination is a result of what Ghandi called *Satyagraha* or truth force. Assertiveness, as a form of Satyagraha, shines a light on the nature of your relationships.

If the other person is not respectful of your wishes, in spite of the fact that you have continued to make your wishes clearly known, then you may need to consider if that relationship is a healthy one for you. Because of your assertiveness, you will know exactly where you stand and you are then in a position to make an informed choice about what to do next.

Persistent assertiveness gives the other person the benefit of the doubt and brings clarity to the situation. Not every one will live up to your consideration, but your assertion will illuminate the truth of who is truly respectful to you and who isn't.

TAKE OWNERSHIP BY STARTING
YOUR ASSERTION WITH "I"

The next assertive skill follows directly from step one – answering the question: what do I want in this situation? Assertive communications start with an "I" statement. Now that you've identified what you want, you can take ownership and responsibility for trying to obtain it. Starting your sentences with "I" clearly places the ownership where it belongs.

The "I" statement is a way of pointing the finger at yourself, rather than at the other person. Literally pointing the finger at yourself, in conjunction with the spoken "I," gives the interaction an entirely different feel from starting with "*you should...*" – one that is not accusatory, but instead conveys ownership for your complaint or request.

Try this experiment. Point your finger at someone and say: "You should..."

Now, point your finger at yourself and say: "I would like..."

Feel the difference? Do you get the sense of how the conversation is likely to end up in two very different places? Notice that there was no topic?

Telling the other person that they *should* be... implies that they are failing somehow as a human being. They should be more... but obviously they're not. The natural reaction to hearing the message that you are failing as a person is to defend yourself. You disagree. This escalates the conflict, which was the very thing you were trying to avoid. The issue then gets lost in the defensive reaction.

From the point of view of the other person, it is much easier to hear "*I would like...*" rather than "*you should...*" This deceptively simple tactic – beginning your sentences with I instead of you – has a powerful influence in determining the subsequent trajectory of the interaction. You are more likely to go down an assertive path rather than an aggressive one.

Starting your sentence with "I" means that you take ownership and responsibility for what you want. Conversely, if you start your communication with "you..." and then follow this with "*should,*" "*never*" or "*always,*" you have instantly slid into aggression – with the first two words out of your mouth! You don't need to even finish the statement to find yourself suddenly in the middle of a disagreement. It's not about the issue; it's about the communication. You can always agree to disagree, but no one likes to be dismissed or belittled.

If you start your sentence with "*you never...*" and then point your finger at the other person, prepare for an escalation, as they now have to defend themself from what is experienced as a put down. This is not very effective, unless you are looking to start a fight. The actual complaint is then lost in the ensuing conflict.

Does that mean you should never use the word *you* in any assertive communication? No, of course not. That would leave you tied in knots trying to analyze every word coming out of your mouth. Just start your sentences with *I* rather than *you* and you will find yourself going down a different path: one that is more likely to be assertive and less likely to be blaming. If you find yourself using a lot of 'you's' make a deliberate effort to go back to the I's. Put the emphasis on what you want rather than on what the other person should do.

"I don't like it when you are late. I feel disrespected." rather than:

"You're late again. You're so disrespectful."

Both sentences convey a similar message but one communicates ownership and expresses authentically how you feel and what you don't like. The other communicates judgement and blame. Empowerment comes from proactively stating your feelings and thoughts rather than reacting to the other person. You stand up for yourself rather than put the other person down. The focus is on you as you identify and express your intention; that's self-direction. Starting your communication with 'I' helps to keep the emphasis where it needs to be in order to feel empowered.

DON'T SOFTEN THE BLOW

If you are uncomfortable in stating what you want or saying no to a request, you may attempt to 'soften the blow' of your assertion. For example, you may say things like:

"I know this is probably an inconvenience."

"If it wouldn't be too much trouble."

"I'm really sorry to ask you this."

"Maybe I could help you find someone else to do that for you."

These attempts to soften the blow undermine your assertion and imply that you don't actually have the right to say what you are saying. That confuses your message. What are you really up to? Do you have the right to ask that or not? If you state what you want in a clear and specific way, there is no hidden agenda or undermining of your rights.

Softening the blow is based on an over concern with the other person's feelings. You try to take responsibility for them, but ultimately you are responsible for your stuff and they are responsible for their stuff. Being clear, specific and direct about what you want is the most respectful way of communicating. Softening the blow is actually condescending as it implies that the other person is not capable of handling the situation.

Examples of clear assertion, without softening the blow, are:

"I want you to do the dishes before 7:00 this evening."

"I would like you to pay me back the $100 I lent you, before Friday."

"I would like it if you were more affectionate. For example, I like it when you hug me when you come home from work. I also like it when you hold my hand when we are going for a walk."

ONLY BRING UP ONE ISSUE AT A TIME

It is all too easy to bring up multiple issues in the heat of the moment:

"You left your clothes on the floor again! What do think I am, you're maid?" And you haven't even started your home-work. It's nearly 11:00! You're going to fail your classes! Do I have to think of everything for you?"

The sudden outpouring of a list of complaints happens if you have historically been passive in the relationship, swal-lowing resentments over time to avoid conflict and to not rock the boat. In doing so, though, you collect a litany of

unexpressed grievances, each one adding fuel to the smoul-
dering fire of resentment. The present conflict then becomes
an opportunity to finally unload all of those things that you
have been keeping to yourself. However, bringing up an
entire list of complaints only dilutes the current issue and
results in a defensive reaction from the other person. No one
wants to hear a list of his or her perceived shortcomings. It's
hard enough to hear just one.

The assertive approach is to deal with only one issue at
a time. Stick to one issue and one issue only. That's why it's
so important to identify the main issue to begin with; what
is your most important concern? Go with that concern and
leave the other issues for now, even if they are also important
to you. If you bring in two issues, the probability of solving
either diminishes rapidly. Accept that you can't solve everything at once. Realistically, it takes time and effort to build
a relationship and, in fact, you could argue that working
through an issue together *is* the relationship.

Over time, issues will tend to be dealt with more immediately as they arise. This prevents any festering resentments
in the relationship and brings you closer to the people you
care about. You discover that you can talk about issues as
they emerge and then work through them. Doing so builds
mutual respect, trust and intimacy, thus deepening your connections with others and enhancing your feelings of social
empowerment. You find your assertive voice.

SORTING THE ISSUES

Sorting the issues is another essential assertive skill. But,
what exactly is the issue? Fortunately, you already know, as
you took the time to clarify your answer to the question:

"What do I want in this situation?"

The answer to that question is the issue. Everything else
isn't. So sorting the issue means coming back to the point:

"I would like this..."

Sorting the issues means that you persistently steer the conversation back to the issue at hand. You stay focused on that issue; you don't get side-tracked or tangled up in other issues.

What if the other person changes the subject? For example:

"Oh, yeah? Well you're just like your mother!" or:

"But I really need the money because I'm in a jam!" or:

"How can you say no? You're so selfish. You only think about yourself!"

None of these things are the issue. They are attempts to deflect away from the issue or to manipulate you, through guilt, into changing your stance. How can you deal with these deflections?

One strategy is to simply ignore the irrelevancy. Are you just like your mother? Is that a bad thing? Is it relevant? So you may just let the comment bounce off you and restate the issue that you have identified as being important:

"Well, what's important to me here is this..."

If you find the other person's statements rude or disrespectful, you may first set limits with the disrespect and then reiterate the issue:

"I don't appreciate it when you say I'm selfish. I find that very disrespectful. However, what were talking about is..."(restating the issue).

Another strategy for dealing with deflections is called empathic assertion, which will be elaborated in a later chapter. If you genuinely have a sense of empathy for the person you can reflect that concern, then restate the issue.

"I understand that you're in a jam. It sounds like you're feeling pretty desperate. I need to be clear, though: I am not going to lend you money."

Sorting the issues means that you bring the focus back to what's important. You might briefly address the tangent that the person has gone off on, but then you conclude by restating the issue you have identified.

CONGRUENCE BETWEEN THE VERBAL AND THE NON-VERBAL

Congruence is another aspect of assertive communication. What exactly is congruence? Congruence represents a state of harmony between diverse elements. In assertiveness, the non-verbal and the verbal elements need to be in harmony with each other. When they are harmonious, they both tell the same story, but with different voices.

The verbal communication consists of the words that you select in order to communicate your message. Non-verbal communication includes the tone of your voice, your posture, gestures, eye contact, facial expressions, physical proximity and movements. What you say and how you say it both communicate a message, but you tend to believe the non-verbal communication over the words. So, when there is incongruence between the non-verbal and the verbal, your anxiety goes up in the face of the mixed message that you are receiving and you look to the non-verbal to clarify the 'truth' of what is going on.

"I can't work late tonight because I have to be home for my kids."

If you say this (verbally) clear and assertive statement, while staring at the floor, shuffling from foot to foot and wringing your hands, you create incongruence between the verbal and non-verbal aspects of your communication. Now there are two messages rather than just one.

The statement itself clearly states what you want and gives a reason that is true and honest. The implication is that you have the right to state this request and that you fully expect it to be honored. The non-verbal message is quite a different matter; it implies that you don't actually have the right to make the request, that you are doing something wrong by asking and that you fully expect that you will be turned down. That's the exact opposite of the words! These two messages are clearly not in harmony; instead they are glaringly incongruent. There is a cacophony to the communication that is not pleasing.

It is human nature to look to the non-verbal in order to ascertain the 'truth' of the situation. Therefore, the mixed message can come across as duplicitous, the implication being that you have some sort of a hidden agenda. You are trying to get away with something:

"He's acting as though it is wrong to ask me this, or to expect that I will allow it, so what's this all about really? What is he up to?"

A congruent communication emerges when the non-verbal is in harmony with the verbal, when both communicate precisely the same thing. For example, saying:

"I can't work tonight because I have to be home for my kids," while making good eye contact, having upright body posture, standing at an appropriate distance and appearing relaxed and at ease. There are no crossed messages; everything you do and say lines up to tell exactly the same story. Your verbal and non-verbal voices are in harmony. There is no hidden agenda lurking in the shadows. It is very difficult to misinterpret an assertive communication when the words are so clear and specific and the non-verbal communication is in full support of those words. The clarity of the communication makes the message harder to argue with, because you have provided no openings for deflecting the issue.

THE POWER OF MAINTAINING AN ASSERTIVE STANCE

Another assertive skill is maintaining an assertive stance throughout the interaction. Assertive communication represents a mutuality of rights and respect. You don't go one-up or one-down in relationship to the other person during the course of the interaction. You maintain a position of mutual respect and equality, regardless of the position that the other person takes. The message is:

"You have rights and so do I."

Each subsequent communication consistently projects this same mutuality and equality. If the other person raises his voice or starts to use demeaning words, you don't respond in kind. You simply maintain your assertive stance. In doing so, your actions emerge from your intention, rather than being a reaction to the other person's escalation. Even when you point out the other person's lack of respect, you do so respectfully. You neither raise your voice nor soften it to a whisper. You persist in presenting a respectful attitude and posture.

Your consistency during the interaction reflects a respect for your self and for the other person. Maintaining the same assertive stance is a powerful tool in any interaction, but especially so when the other person escalates. Not only does it take two to be a doormat, it takes two to escalate a conflict.

Satyagraha

Maintaining a consistent and respectful assertive stance illuminates the inappropriateness of any aggressive response. In an extraordinary and extreme example of the power of maintaining a respectful stance, Gandhi used a similar technique to set in motion the events that would bring about the emancipation of India from British rule.

The Indian people were used as slave labour to carry water from the sea to boilers that would evaporate the ocean water and leave the salt residue. Then, the Indian laborers would carry the salt to bins where the salt would be stored for sale. When the laborers needed salt, they would have to line up and pay the English colonialists in order to receive the salt.

Gandhi noted the injustice in this and pointed out that the salt came from the land of India and that the salt was obtained, processed and transported by their labour and therefore was rightly theirs. Gandhi formulated a plan of non-violent resistance. One morning hundreds of Indians lined up to get their salt. The person at the head of the line would politely say: "I want my salt." The soldiers would demand money for the salt, but the person would simply reiterate politely: "I would like my salt." The soldiers became angry and lashed out, striking the laborers until they fell to the ground. The next person in line would then start the same process. At some point, though, the soldiers could no longer continue beating the men and refused to follow the orders to do so. These events were filmed and shown to an outraged world and the end of English rule over India began.

Although this strategy has been referred to as passive resistance – to discriminate it from violent resistance – assertive-resistance better describes the interactions. The courageous Indian laborers maintained an assertive stance in the face of physical aggression, acting on their clearly reasonable rights. Maintaining that position, even in the face of physical assault, led to enormous social and political changes that culminated in India reclaiming power over it's own territory and goods.

Gandhi himself preferred the Indian term *Satyagraha* to the English phrase of passive resistance. He felt that the word passive implied weakness, whereas the term Satyagraha translates, much more powerfully, as: truth force. The spirit of Satyagraha is to make the truth known and visible, without attacking the other person, in the supposition that this action would ultimately lead to a more just world. The concept of Satyagraha is consistent with the philosophy, values and methods of assertiveness: to stand firm, to make the truth known and to maintain a respectful stance.

Persistence Over Time

Persistence in assertiveness means that you maintain an assertive stance not only within an interaction, but also over time. You persist in a specific communication and also in your relationship. For example, if you have asked someone for a change in their behaviour and a few weeks later they fall back in to the old way, it is important to persevere in your assertiveness:

"Remember last week when we talked about this and you agreed to put the dishes away after supper? You have been doing a great job of it, but this weekend you forgot. Could you put them away now?"

"Remember last week, when I asked you to fill up the car before you brought it home? I found that it's nearly empty so I would like you to go fill it up now."

Maintaining mutual respect and equality reflects an assertive and empowered way of being-in-the-world. If you have set limits with some behaviour but now you find it recurring, you call the person on it and you do this in a respectful way.

Persistence over time teaches others to treat you with respect and to take your concerns seriously, because you do. It shapes your relationships as you build positive and mutually respectful ways of being with others over the long run. Reminders become less necessary over time as others come to know what is expected of them and that you take your requests seriously.

THE RIGHT TIME AND PLACE

Context can make all the difference in determining whether a communication is assertive. For example, a supervisor can give you a performance appraisal and communicate that critique using assertive skills, but still not be truly assertive. How might that happen?

One example would be the situation where your performance feedback was given in front of your co-workers. In that context, any negative aspects of the feedback could readily have the effect of publicly humiliating or embarrassing you and thus the communication would fall into the passive-aggressive category. The appraisal ostensibly has the purpose of facilitating your development, but the result is that instead you feel put down. Context is immensely important in ensuring that your communications are as assertive as you intended them to be. Being sensitive to the surroundings in which your interactions take place is a thoughtful and considerate part of being assertive.

The most respectful context for assertion is face-to-face, in a quiet place and without an audience. This allows for full attention to be devoted to the communication without distraction. The emotional and physical states of the person are also important considerations. If they are exhausted, sick or have to be somewhere else in the next few minutes, that is not the most respectful context for dealing with some assertive issue. If the available time to address the issue is short, mention that upfront and check with the person if that will be sufficient in order to discuss the concern. These guidelines help in respecting the other person and in respecting the issue that you are bringing up by giving it the time and care it deserves.

THE MEDIUM IS THE MESSAGE: CONTEXTS FOR ASSERTION

Face to Face Communication

In face-to-face communication, you see the other person and they see you; that means you both get immediate and ongoing feedback. You observe each other's physical reactions to the conversation and those non-verbals bring a wealth of information to the communication. How close you are standing to the other person, your facial expressions, tone of voice, body posture and eye contact all add important information to what is being said and shape the meaning of your communication.

The face-to-face communication ideally occurs in an unhurried scenario and without the presence of an audience. That is the most respectful forum and also makes for the least distractions. However, sometimes, assertive situations arise suddenly and unexpectedly, while others are observing. If at all possible, pull the person aside in order to have a more private conversation. You are trying to deal with the issue rather than embarrass the person in front of others. However, if someone confronts you publically, you may need to respond immediately in spite of the presence of others.

Videotelephony: Skype/FaceTime

Video-telephonic communication such as Skype and FaceTime adds elements of non-verbal feedback, in the form of facial expressions, to the audio communication of telephone. The presence of facial reactions within the interaction is an important modulator of any emotional expressions that go along with the communication. Facial expressions convey a wealth of emotional information, perhaps more than all other non-verbals. Imagine a conversation where you could only see the rest of the body and not the face!

Phone Communication

In voice-to-voice communication over the phone, the non-verbal expression in the voice is included in the communication and adds shades of meaning to the words. However, phone-calls have their own significant problematic areas. All of the information is aural. A brief silence on the telephone can be interpreted as inattention, boredom or a desire to end the phone-call. Natural pauses in the conversation that are typically part of a relaxed and comfortable way of being with someone in person, suddenly become fodder for interpretation when the voice is the solitary stimulus in the phenomenal field. The mind scans, interprets and utilizes those cues that are available. Less cues equal more interpretations.

Letter Writing

The art of letter writing, perhaps on the verge of extinction, had unique strengths. You could express your self in a great deal of depth, choosing your words and thoughts with care and elaborating comprehensively on the points you raised. Try reading letters to the editor from a hundred years ago. It will be immediately apparent that we have lost the *art* of letter writing in the present day.

On the other hand, letter writing is very much a one-sided conversation. It might be weeks before the other person responds and the issues may have dimmed with the passage of time. Letter writing also lacks non-verbal aspects that provide depth and meaning to the correspondence.

E-mail

E-mail tends to have the same problems as letter writing with the exception of the speed of response by the other person. However, the instantaneous nature of email as a form of communication can create it's own problems. You can fire off your response without the benefit of thoughtful and considered editing. This is similar to cursing out the other drivers on the road without their physical presence giving you pause to modulate your words. Now, with email, you have a send button to move your rant out into the world.

Email is devoid of the non-verbal aspects that might channel the communication towards an assertive rather than an aggressive or passive-aggressive direction. The development of Emoticons is an attempt to rectify this oversight, but they are a poor substitute for the real thing.

Emailing has become ubiquitous in business as a form of communication and so emails are used daily in an attempt to deal with assertive issues. Therefore, following is a list of guidelines for using e-mail to deal with assertive situations.

E-mail Guidelines for Assertive Communication

1) Only use e-mail as a last resort when dealing with situations involving conflict, emotion or for complex issues. Then, do so at your peril and with a decreased expectation for successful resolution.

2) Never hit the reply button in anger. If you do find your self raising your finger to stab at the reply button with an angry retort, use that as a cue to remember: *never hit the reply button in anger.* Slowly back out of the 'reply now' situation. Leave your computer desk and go for coffee. Meditate. Breathe.

When you are lit up in the heat of anger, the accompanying charge of adrenalin will make it more difficult to maintain an assertive stance over the course of the interaction. It becomes all too easy to slide into aggression. Let your anger inform, but not direct, your response.

Give your self some time to process your emotional reaction and ponder the meaning of the communication: What is the person really saying? What is the key thing that I feel angry about? What do I want in this situation?

3) Try not to add your own non-verbal aspects to the e-mail that you have received. When you read e-mail, your mind fills in the non-verbal parts in order to help you 'get' the message. The sarcastic tone that you are hearing in your head may not

have actually been there. The particular word that jumps out at you may not have been given extra emphasis by the sender.

Here is an example of how a written communication can be misinterpreted. A young woman in an assertiveness group was deeply offended and hurt when I wrote the following question on the white board:
"What do you want?"
I was perplexed as to how this (written) communication could elicit such a reaction, until she told me that she heard it as:
"What do *you* want?"
She also added a contemptuous tone of voice in her mind, so that the message then became:
"You have no right to ask for anything! Just who the hell do you think you are?"
That was clearly *not* the message I was trying to communicate in my brief (four syllable) communication, in fact, quite the contrary. Yet the meaning was turned 180 degrees into the very opposite of what I had intended, simply by imagining a certain tone of voice underlining one of the words.

Try re-reading an apparently offending communication without enriching it by adding non-verbal aspects. Is it still offending? Remember that in assertiveness, you try to give the other person the benefit of the doubt.

4) Be brief, clear and precise when sending your e-mail communication. Re-read it before you push the send button. Ask your self: can my message be misinterpreted? Am I, in fact being sarcastic or passive-aggressive? Is there an edge? If so, change the communication so that it is more assertive. Remove the edge. There should be no 'reading between the lines' communication inferred. Don't *imply* things, but *do* state exactly what you mean. Recall that even the simplest message can (and will) be filtered through the mind and past experiences of the reader.

5) If you think some part of your communication is open to interpretation, restate the message by saying it again in a different way, so that the meaning is elaborated and reiterated. Example:

"So when I write: 'What do you want?' on the board, what I am asking you to do is to take the time to think about what you actually *do* want in the situation. What's the most important thing you would like to get out of that situation?"

In this example the receiver would have to work very hard in order to sustain any negative interpretations of the communication.

6) If the issue is emotional, complex or involves conflict, consider at least picking up the phone to talk with the person directly and to clarify the key issues. Better, of course, would be a face-to-face meeting, unhurried, with no audience. Context becomes especially important if you sense that emotions are starting to impact the interaction. Simply adding the non-verbal expression of your voice to the interaction can serve to dramatically alter the outcome and allow you to work through issues and diffuse the situation.

Texting

Don't use texting in an effort to resolve a conflict. Texting is more relevant to brief, factual exchanges such as setting up a place to meet and so on. Texting lends itself very well to positive communications such as "way to go!" "Love you lots!" "Miss you!" Keep it brief and positive.

14
Speaking With an Assertive Voice

"Speak your truth quietly and clearly."

The Desiderata

L earning the key elements of assertion provides you with an excellent set of tools that are foundational for social empowerment. These are some frequently encountered situations where you can practice speaking with an assertive voice: saying no; asking for what you want; expressing thoughts and feelings; giving and receiving compliments and criticism.

SAYING NO

Saying no to what you don't want is a fundamental assertive act. It is also one of the situations that can readily evoke feelings of guilt and anxiety. The hardest part of saying no is not so much learning the skill, but rather overcoming any internal barriers. Guilt and anxiety arise from belief systems and internal rules that promote a passive, one-down position in your relationships.

Do say no. Include the word 'no' in your communication instead of trying to soften the blow by dancing around the actual answer to the request. The answer is no, so be clear.

Do be brief, *no* is a straightforward answer to a question, don't complicate it with excessive discussion in an attempt to protect the person's feelings. Don't soften the blow. He has the right to ask for what he wants (that's his stuff) and you have the right to say no (that's your stuff). You *both* have rights: that's the mutuality and equality implicit in assertiveness. That way there is no resentment:

"He really has some nerve asking me that!"

The skill of saying no is also evident in what you *don't* do in the situation: don't apologize (unless you actually have done something wrong); don't give a list of reasons for saying no in order to justify your assertion; don't offer to take on the responsibility for finding someone else to meet the request because you can't; and last, but certainly not least, don't say yes when you mean no.

What about the guilt that arises from saying no? There is no guilt/anxiety if you truly allow yourself the *right* to turn down a request. Of course, this is easier said than done when guilt is your constant companion. The good news is that it doesn't have to be. In order to overcome dysfunctional guilt, you will need to do certain things differently. Most importantly, you will need to persist in being assertive, in spite of the guilt.

Why shouldn't you apologize if you turn down a request? What's wrong with: "I'm really sorry that I can't babysit your four kids this weekend."

First of all, are you truly "really sorry?" If not, then this answer is not honest and authentic. Instead you are being passive by misrepresenting how you actually feel.

Secondly, when you apologize you are giving yourself the message that you are doing something wrong. An apology is essentially an admission of guilt. In voicing the apology you reinforce the belief that you do not have the right to turn down the request. Saying no will not get any easier in the future; it will get much harder.

Thirdly, the other person can also understand your apology as an admission that you are doing something wrong. That apology provides fodder for more arguments and increased pressure to give in to the request:

"I'm really sorry I can't go out with you this week."

"That's OK, how's next week?"

"Well, I'm busy then too – you know, my crazy schedule. I'm really sorry."

"Well, you can be sorry, but maybe you need to organize your self a little better. Let's get together and I can show you how to be more organized."

What about giving reasons and justifications for saying no? What could be possibly wrong with that? Isn't that just being sensitive? These are all good questions. Social empowerment through assertiveness is, after all, about mutual respect, so why not explain your self?

If you do give a reason for saying no – and there is no universal requirement of this – then *give only one reason and make it the real, honest reason*. The reason can be simply: "because I don't want to."

The problem with giving multiple explanations and justifications is that the focus can easily shift away from the no and onto the justification.

"Hey, I could use a quick lift over to my girlfriend's place. I see your car is parked outside."

"I can't drive you. I don't have much gas in the car."

"That's OK, I'll put $5 of gas in your car when we get there. It's only about twenty miles."

"Well, uh, I have to pick up my kids."

"We'll swing by and pick them up on the way. Hey, why don't we bring them with us, the more the merrier."

"But I'm not picking them up until 5:00."

"No problem-o, we can go for a drive while we wait."

Here's the same example without offering justifications:

"Hey, I could use a quick lift over to my girlfriend's place. I see your car is parked outside."

"No, I can't help you."

"C'mon, it won't take long, it's only twenty miles."

"No."

"Why not? I thought we were friends. I'd help you out in a minute if you asked me."

"I don't want to drive you. My answer is no and I'd appreciate it if you accepted that."

Here's another example:

"I want to borrow the books you used for the lecture."

"No, I don't lend them out."

"You don't understand. It's no problem; I'm a friend of your colleague. I'll give the books back to him when I'm finished with them."

"No."

"No? What do you mean, no? I just need them for a few weeks!"

"No."

"Well why not?"

"Because I don't want to lend them out."

The above examples illustrate aspects of the assertive skill of saying no: being brief; saying no; not apologizing; and only giving one reason that is the true and honest reason. The reason offered and reiterated is:

"I don't want to lend them out."

This is not an explanation, but is simply another way of stating your right to say no to a request. You have the right to say no without explaining or justifying yourself. You simply assert, in a respectful way, your choice to say no to things you do not want: yes, he has the right to ask and, yes, you have the right to say no. That way, there are no lingering resentments or feelings of guilt.

ASKING FOR WHAT YOU WANT

Not only do you have the right to say no, but you also have the right to ask for what you want – to make requests of others. You don't necessarily have the right to *get* what you want, but you do have the right to *ask*. Others have these same rights.

In making a request, it is important to be clear and specific about what it is that you asking. Doing so respects the other person's right to know exactly what it is that they are being asked and then they can make an informed decision in response to your request.

A soldier once said:

"Assertiveness won't work in the military, it's an aggressive organization and that's how the chain of command works! Assertion might work for you civilians, but it just won't fly in the army."

He was chronically angry with the soldiers who worked under his command. He watched them and observed that they would not do much work during the day, but then would fly into a flurry of activity at the last moment in order to achieve the day's tasks, usually in the last hour of work. The officer would spend the entire day steaming mad at these soldiers, but wouldn't say anything to them. Instead, he found ways to punish then indirectly. He would vent his frustration by assigning them other work at the last minute. The soldiers under his command developed resentment and so the environment had become very chilly and unpleasant. Nobody was happy with how things were going and morale had hit an all time low.

The officer's behavior can be seen not as aggressive, but rather as passive and passive-aggressive. In exploring what he wanted in the situation, he started with a vague request that focused on what he didn't want and involved a put-down:

"I want them to stop being so @#** lazy."

He was encouraged to be more specific and start his request with an "I" statement and he eventually arrived at this statement:

"I would like them to finish storing the supplies before noon."

He used an "I" statement, identified a key issue that was important to him, and was specific and clear in his statement, in contrast with his initial formulation. If he had gone with his first thought (stop being so @#** lazy!), it is unlikely that the work environment would have improved.

Fortunately, in spite of his initial skepticism, he did try out this assertive communication on his next morning at work. To his amazement, the team sprang into action and immediately carried out his request, all of this work being accomplished well before the lunch hour. He was so pleased with his crew (maybe they're not so lazy after all?) that he actually complimented them on their work. They brightened in response. They were happy to be able to do the work being asked of them and to finally know what the expectations were. The officer continued to practice these skills, the soldiers morale and work habits improved and the job environment became much more pleasant for all.

His assertion in making a clear and specific request had the effect of not only respecting his own rights to have the work done, but also the soldier's rights to have clear guidelines as to what was expected from them. The chain of command was actually strengthened through assertive communication.

The core elements of assertive behavior, such as the use of "I" statements and being specific and clear are important when making a request. Here's an example of an aggressive way of making a request:

"You never clean up after your self. You always leave such a mess and then I have to clean it up! What do you think I am, your maid?"

This example represents the blaming, shaming way of making a request. It puts you one-up in the relationship. You're a good person (hard working, value cleanliness) and they are not (lazy and assuming incorrectly that you are their maid.) Notice the "you should…", "you never…", "you always…" statements; these imply blame and failure. The message is that "you are a bad person." Nobody wants to hear that and so of course the reaction is disagreement, the exact opposite of what you were hoping for. If an argument ensues, it will be more about *how* you are communicating rather than *what* you are communicating.

Here's an assertive example of the same request:

"I would like you to put your dishes in the dishwasher when you're done. It would save me a lot of work later."

In this example you are taking ownership for what you want by starting with an "I" statement and by being clear and specific about what you would like from the other person. You give one reason and it is the true and honest reason for the request. Now, it is much easier for the other person to hear what you are saying. There's less noise. There are no competing messages about being a bad person, just the clear request about the change that you would like to happen.

EXPRESSING THOUGHTS AND FEELINGS

Assertion is not always about problems or conflict; it's also about simply expressing yourself and letting others get to know you in doing so. Expressing your emotions and opinions allows you to practice having a voice in your relationships. It's an important step in building intimacy.

Expressing thoughts and feelings is an excellent starting place to begin your practice of assertiveness. Conflict situations can be more emotionally intense, difficult situations. Practice self-expression in non-conflict situations first and then, when you have mastered those skills, move on to more challenging situations. If you were playing basketball, you wouldn't wait until the big game to practice and then hope the skills would magically materialize. Instead, you would practice your lay-ups and jump shots in the gym in a less-pressured way. Then, in the big game, the skills that you have practiced hundreds of times would kick in. The same applies to learning any new skill, whether it is physical or social.

You can practice expressing your thoughts and emotions on a daily basis. Use "I" statements and be clear and specific. Here are some examples:

"I feel sad when I hear that music. It reminds me of my mother. I miss her."

"I think there is too much negative news in the newspaper."

"I feel tired today."

"I am really looking forward to going on that trip."

These are examples of expressing thoughts and feelings that are not about solving problems. They just convey how you feel and what you think at the moment. They are honest, clear and direct without putting anyone down and thus meet the definition of assertiveness.

Practicing these expressive skills will help you gain a level of comfortableness in having a voice. It will also help you gain self-knowledge and self-awareness. In order to express these statements, you will have to take the time to ask yourself: how do I feel right now? What do I think about this particular event? Thus, you are practicing the very important art of tuning in to your self. As a result, your feelings and thoughts become more accessible to you, even in the midst of unexpected situations. It makes spontaneous assertiveness more likely to happen in the future:

"You know, I was assertive in that situation and only realized it afterwards. It just came out of me."

GOOD COACHING: THE ART OF FEEDBACK

Good coaching means that you give criticism in a way that is helpful; the feedback you give is likely to be heard and utilized. Good coaching results in skill enhancement, as the person is able to use the coaching to improve their performance. There are two key aspects to good coaching: identifying what the coachee is doing right and identifying one thing that they could improve. These two elements of coaching are also highly effective in self-coaching.

Identifying precisely what it is that you are doing right is crucial to consolidating new learning. If you can't identify what you are doing correctly, then you are likely to keep trying alternative behaviors. The perfect exemplar that you have been striving for comes and goes without notice, disappearing from your memory and from your skill repertoire.

When you do recognize good examples of a skill, you can build your subsequent efforts on that foundation. You have a model for what an outstanding example of the skill might look like and you use that as a guide for your future efforts.

COACHING OTHERS

Giving feedback that draws your attention to what you are doing right (examples of skill mastery) is a core skill in coaching, regardless of whether the skill is physical, behavioral, social or cognitive. In sports, psychologists coach athletes in recognizing moments of peak performance. If you are golfing and you hit the perfect drive, you learn to stop and take a moment to vividly recall what just happened. You take a deep breath, close your eyes and bring up the memory of the drive in as much detail as possible. You tune in to the physical posture you assumed just before the swing and how it felt in your body from start to finish. You familiarize yourself with the posture of success. You visualize every second of the swing, from raising the club to the follow through, in its entirety. This will help you to be able to recreate the experience in the future. Good coaches in sports are well aware of this fundamental coaching method, yet it is rare to see this skill applied in a non-sports context. Good coaching can apply to all aspects of life.

There is a phenomenon in psychology called *behavioral drift* that represents a natural tendency towards drifting away from a demonstrated skill over time. If you are not fully aware of the desired response, it is difficult to notice the drift that naturally occurs from that response. Awareness of behavioral drift facilitates the ability to self-correct, which is an important part of mastering and maintaining a skill over time. Self-correction requires that you notice deviations from your goal and then make the necessary adjustments to return to the desired skill level. Instead of berating yourself for being less than perfect, you use that information to adjust and improve your skills. Part of peak performance is noticing when your skills are sub-optimal and then upping your game.

Once you have become fully aware of what you are doing right, the good coach can then draw your attention to one thing you could improve. Note the specific wording of the phrase:

"One thing you could improve", rather than:

"One thing you did wrong."

This subtle difference in words has huge implications. One is the language of solutions and success, while the other wording implies blame and failure. One points out your lack of mastery, and the other directs your attention to how you might achieve that mastery; that's the good coaching.

In the assertive skill of giving feedback, you begin by letting the other person know what they are doing right. Here's an example of good coaching:

"I liked the way you used 'I' statements in your assertion. That made it feel like you were taking ownership for the issue, rather than blaming the other person. I thought you also did a good job of sorting the issues and bringing the conversation back to the issue at hand. By doing that, you really kept the focus on what you wanted. I think one thing you could improve is to make more eye contact during the interaction."

Notice that the successful elements are identified first, followed by one area for improvement. Identifying what the person is getting right helps to build confidence and that makes it easier to hear about the things that could be improved. Knowing that you are getting some of it right makes it easier to tolerate the fact that you are not yet perfect.

The feedback for improvement is specific, clear and solution based: make more eye contact. If you agree with the criticism, the solution is obvious. The feedback only brought up one area for improvement. Even if there are several things that could be improved, it is wise to only mention one. If you are overloaded with feedback, it is more difficult to integrate the criticism. Deal with one thing at a time and when that part of the skill is integrated, then move on to the next thing to be improved.

This is a good place to practice all the aspects of positive self-talk, whether you are coaching yourself or someone else: use an encouraging tone of voice, positive language and solution-based feedback.

BEING COACHED

If you on the receiving end of the coaching, start by making sure that you understand the feedback. This is a good place for empathic reflection, which is elaborated more fully in the following chapter. You can paraphrase the criticism, without agreeing or disagreeing:

"So you liked my "I" statements and how I kept the focus, but you think I could've looked at the person more directly."

"Yeah, exactly! I thought you had a tendency to look down when you were speaking and I thought that took away a little bit from what you were saying."

Notice how paraphrasing the criticism resulted in agreement (yeah, exactly!) and in more elaboration of the feedback.

In the above example, the coaching is quite specific. In situations where the criticism isn't clear, ask for clarification so that you can fully understand it. Don't jump into disagreeing with poorly worded criticism, even if the criticism feels negative and unfair.

Here's an example of less than optimal coaching as a manager gives performance feedback to an employee:

"You really should be more responsible. You can't just do whatever you like, you know! We're all part of a team and you need to be a team player."

"You want me to show more responsibility and to be more of a team player. Can you tell me specifically what you mean by that?"

"Yeah, I need you to help out on the new project. Mary brought you some work last week and you told her you were too busy to do it. You're letting the whole team down. Like I said, you can't just do whatever you want!"

"You would have preferred it if I had stopped working on the project that I had been working on and started on the new project instead?"

Notice that, up to this point, the employee has neither agreed nor disagreed with any of the criticism, but he has tried to clarify exactly what is being asked of him.

The employee is trying to shift the coaching into a potentially more helpful form of criticism. The quality of the coaching would be improved if the manager was more specific and avoided these vague and blaming statements:

"You need to be more responsible",

"You can't just do whatever you like", and

"You have to be a team player."

All of these criticisms are unclear, imply some degree of personal failure and start with the word you. That is the language of escalation and dominance. It's hard to hear this criticism without becoming defensive because of the aggressive manner in which it's presented. Even if the employee decided to accept this coaching, it is not at all clear what you might do differently.

It is assertive to set limits with inappropriate or disrespectful parts of the criticism, without outright dismissing the criticism in its entirety. There may be some helpful feedback in the communication, once things are clarified and brought more out in the open:

"I find it disrespectful when you say I'm not responsible and that I'm not being a team player. That part of your feedback, to me, (points finger at self) feels like a put down. I was taking responsibility for the project that I was working on and setting limits to ensure that that work gets done on time. There's a team involved with that project as well and we are working together to finish the project within the deadlines we have been given. It seems to me that the issue you are identifying is one of prioritizing the work to be done. You would like me to prioritize the projects differently. Is that what you are saying?"

The employee starts most of his sentences with "I", makes clear and specific statements, sets limits with inappropriate criticism and seeks clarity and understanding in the issue that is concerning the manager. The employee maintains an assertive and respectful stance, even when disagreeing with the inappropriate aspects of the feedback. He neither escalates nor becomes submissive in his response to the manager. Instead, he insists on being treated respectfully while maintaining a respectful attitude towards the manager.

15
Advanced Assertive Voice

*"Deep understanding is the most precious gift
one can give to another."*

Carl Rogers

EMPATHY AND EMPATHIC-ASSERTION

Empathic-assertion is one of the more complex assertive skills. It is also clearly linked to the philosophy of assertiveness in representing a mutuality and equality of respect in relationships. Empathic-assertion takes into account the positions of both people in the interaction.

EMPATHY

In order to understand empathic assertion, it is helpful to first understand the concept of empathy. Empathy represents the ability to put your self into someone else's shoes: to identify with and correctly understand the other person's feelings and point of view. Empathy is enormously important in social interactions while the converse – a lack of empathy for others

– represents a significant deficit in human relations. It is associated with sociopathy.

Empathy is now recognized as one of the most significant factors in emotional intelligence (EQ) and is highly associated with success and leadership abilities in many careers. Empathy for others is a key factor in facilitating social engagement, resilience in the face of stressful and traumatic events and in the ability to maintain good mental health. Empathy is the glue that binds society together: our ability to imagine what an experience is like for the other person and thus to have compassion for that person. Empathy is what allows us to connect to other human beings and to give and receive social support.

Carl Rogers, in a landmark paper in the field of clinical psychology (Rogers, 1957) detailed what he believed were the necessary and sufficient elements for effective psychotherapy. Not surprisingly, empathy was high on that list. In fact, empathy and empathic-reflection are fundamental to psychotherapy. Any skilled psychotherapist will employ empathy in order for the client to have a sense of being understood: this therapist *gets* me. If you don't have that sense from your psychotherapist, continue looking for a better fit, because empathy is essential to the therapeutic process, regardless of the form of the psychotherapy being offered.

Empathy can also be thought of as a personality trait, with individuals naturally varying in their ability. Some people are extremely high in empathy, so much so that they take on the pain and suffering of others in a visceral way, feeling the suffering of the other person just as intensely, or perhaps even more so, than the person actually experiencing the pain.

On the other end of the continuum, some people are almost completely lacking in empathy for others and could watch others suffer with no emotional reaction at all. Brain scans of sociopaths reveal that the part of the pre-frontal cortex having to do with empathy is not functioning adequately.

That part of the brain having to do with empathy is shut down and so the sociopath lacks empathy and compassion for others.

Happily, most of us are somewhere in the middle of those extremes, having enough empathy to be able to feel compassion and engage in social support, but not so much as to be overwhelmed by everything we see.

In 2001, I developed a scale to measure empathy and concern for others (the Empathic-Concern Scale,) after noticing that many people with Posttraumatic Stress Disorder (PTSD) appeared to have very high levels of empathy and concern for others. I wondered if high levels of empathic concern for others represented a vulnerability to being traumatized, particularly in situations of witnessing other people being traumatized. For example, the medic in the army, whose motivation and drive is to help and heal others, can be overwhelmed when viewing the results of warfare and genocide through that empathic lens. First responders such as police, military, paramedics and firefighters are often exposed to multiple traumas, as they witness events such as car accidents, deaths, fires, heart attacks and war atrocities.

The main predictor of developing PTSD subsequent to a trauma is the severity/proximity of the traumatic situation. In other words, how severe the trauma is, and how close you are to the center of it, are the most important variables in predicting who gets PTSD after exposure to a trauma.

High levels of empathy can increase *emotional* proximity to a traumatic event. The more you can put yourself in someone else's shoes, the closer you are to the trauma. That's why hearing that your relative was in a car accident is more upsetting than hearing the same news about a stranger.

I suspected that people who had high levels of empathic concern for others would be at increased risk when put in a position where they would be witnessing the effects of traumatic experiences in others. I measured the effects of witnessing the events of 9/11 on television in the week immediately afterwards, and again, six months later. High empathic concern predicted the development of PTSD symptoms in the immediate week following 9/11, but not six months later. High levels of empathy represented a vulnerability to stress in witnessing others being traumatized via the television news reporting the tragic events. However, empathy was also a protective factor in diminishing the effects of exposure over time. Those with higher levels of empathy were more likely to seek out and engage with others, thus eliciting the social support to ameliorate the effects of the trauma over time. Conversely, social withdrawal, after exposure to trauma, is predictive of a poorer outcome and greater likelihood of developing and sustaining PTSD.

I have included the Empathic-Concern Scale in the appendix along with information to help you score your response. The scale takes about five minutes to fill out. Population norms are given in gender-normed percentiles with cut-offs for very high, average and very low. You can use the scoring to determine what percentile you are in and whether you are high, average or low in empathy. For example, the 99th percentile means that your score was higher than 99 percent of people of that gender.

EMPATHIC-ASSERTION

Steven Covey, in his best-selling book, 'The Seven Habits of Highly Effective People' describes one of the habits as:
"First, seek to understand."
There are profound implications in these four words that point to a path for the resolution of human conflicts and for building positive and intimate relationships.

Conflicts do not come from having a different point of view. Rather, conflicts arise from the experience of *not being heard*. You can always agree to disagree, but if you are not being heard, you are likely to feel slighted, frustrated and annoyed. There is a tendency to talk louder when you don't feel heard, as if the situation were simply due to deafness on the other person's part and that more volume will remedy the situation. However, talking louder means that you escalate the interaction. You go one-up. The other person then also has to talk louder in order to regain lost ground.

Not being heard is the driving force behind many escalations in conflicts, whether political or personal. Conversely, the sense of being heard has the effect of de-escalating conflicts. Even more importantly, the feeling of being heard manifests in a sense of safety and trust in the relationship, providing a secure base for exploring differences, resolving issues and strengthening a sense of connection.

Seeking to understand is one thing but *conveying* that understanding to the other person is quite another. First, seek to understand, needs to be followed by: secondly, communicate that understanding. This involves the skill of empathic-assertion. While empathy is the ability to resonate with and *get* the other person, empathic-assertion transmits that knowledge to the person. It is not enough to know what the other person is feeling; you have to let the other person know that you know.

Simply saying:

"I understand how you feel" isn't sufficient and is likely to be met with:

"No, you don't!"

In using the skill of empathic-assertion you 'put your money where your mouth is' as you actually demonstrate to the person that you do indeed grasp the nature of their experience.

For example:

"You must feel so frustrated."

"I bet you're disappointed by that."

"It sounds like you really miss her."

Empathy allows you to resonate with the other person's

emotional state. You tune in to them and identify what they are feeling. Conveying that empathic awareness requires the skill of empathic-reflection.

THE ART OF REFLECTION

Seeking to understand the other person's position requires empathy and listening skills. It is essential to take time and effort to understand the other's position first, without agreeing or disagreeing with that position. Hold off on the agree/disagree part and just stick with attempting to really understand so that you really *get* where the other person is coming from. Conflicts will often resolve themselves through this process with no need to ever go to the agree/disagree part.

The skill of empathic-assertion is based on the art of *reflection* as a form of communication. Reflection involves paraphrasing the words of the other person. The crudest, most basic form would be just to repeat parrot-like, the words of the other person. That form of communication is no less annoying now than it was when your little brother was doing it for hours on end and mom wouldn't make him stop. So, don't parrot – paraphrase.

Paraphrasing requires you to put the other person's thoughts into your own words rather than simply repeating the words that have been expressed. This means that you have to listen to the other person, as completely as possible, rather than half paying attention while you are busy planning a counter-argument.

There are many men who would benefit from practicing the skill of empathic-reflection in their relationships. Males sometimes like to jump into problem solving and fixing things while their spouses may simply desire to feel heard and understood. Men tend to be do-ers, and jump into action, even when listening and reflecting would be a more helpful response. Empathic reflection demonstrates that you understand the other person. It builds intimacy.

There are varying degrees of empathy. In basic levels of empathy you simply restate without adding or changing what was said. More profound levels are evident when you include feelings or thoughts that haven't been expressed verbally at all, but that you sense are part of the person's experience. When you are correct in identifying unspoken feelings, the response will be visible, as the person feels understood. You have proven that you truly understand them, so they feel understood and they know you are listening. They will then start to open up even more as they feel safe within the containment of your empathic understanding. Empathic reflection thus deepens your connection with the other person.

What if you are off target in your refection? What if you make a reflection but you miss the mark? There is good news: you can't really lose when you are attempting empathic-reflection; if you are incorrect the other person will simply clarify what hasn't been conveyed. They sense that you are trying your best to understand.

"It sounds like you're pretty mad about the situation."

"No, I'm not so much angry as I am sad about the whole thing."

He still feels safe as he senses that you are trying to understand him and he has given you more information and clarification to help you correctly attune your empathic response.

Empathic reflection is a powerful tool for resolving conflicts and building intimacy. It is based on the fundamental human need to feel heard and understood. Empathic reflection is experienced as validating whereas agreement alone does not carry that impact. In conflict situations, most people can easily tolerate some degree of difference of opinion. It is much harder to accept not feeling heard.

EMPATHIC-ASSERTION AND SAYING NO

Empathic-assertion can be used as an alternative response to assuming responsibility for someone else's problems. When you are passive, you tend to take on the weight of other people's problems. Empathy offers an assertive option. You can empathize while still setting limits.

An example of a passive response when turning down a request:

"I'm really sorry I can't baby-sit your four children for the weekend, but have you tried phoning Mary? She might be able to do it. Would you like me to call her for you?"

The initial response is to say no to the request. But then, driven by guilt and a need to placate, you volunteer to solve the problem for the person. In doing so, you take on their issues as though they were your own. You feel responsible for their problem.

Assertiveness is about taking responsibility for yourself while letting others take responsibility for themselves. Those are the values of ownership and accountability. Ask yourself this:

"Whose stuff is it anyway?"

An assertive example of saying no and using empathic assertion:

"I can't baby-sit your four children for the weekend. It sounds like you're feeling anxious about what to do this weekend."

The initial response of saying no is followed by an empathic reflection rather than a care-taking response. The person in need of a baby-sitter may not have said she is anxious, but the anxiety is inferred and reflected. If you are wrong, the response is to correct the misaligned resonance:

"No, I'm not anxious, I'm more angry that my boss put me in this position where I have to get a baby-sitter at the last minute."

Even with the 'error' in identifying the emotion, the other person feels heard and understood. No caretaking solutions are offered on the assumption that the other person is fully able to take responsibility for solving their own problem. That's their stuff. You are being a good friend, though, through your empathy for what the other person is going through.

Empathy provides a safe place where the person can work through their issues. New insights often develop and become articulated as you explore your thoughts within the safe containment of feeling heard and understood.

"You know, I'm just realizing how I'm angry at my boss; I think I'll call her and tell her I can't work on the weekend. I didn't really want to do that anyway. Thanks for helping me figure this out."

"But I didn't do anything."

"Yes you did; you listened!"

ASSERTIVENESS IN CHALLENGING SITUATIONS

When Someone Won't Take No For An Answer

Sometimes you are assertive but your assertion is not respected. For example, the other person refuses to take no for an answer. You treat them respectfully, but they don't return the favor. Phone sales people often fall into this category. The nature of their job requires them to be pushy and to not take no for an answer. They might even be reading from a script provided to them, so that whatever way you say no, they have some comeback. Essentially, their job is designed as an instruction manual in exhibiting 'bad faith' in human relationships.

"I'm not interested in your service."

"Can I ask why not?"

"I don't want to get into it, but I'm not interested."

"But, it's free for the first thirty days! How can you not want something that's free?"

"As I said, I'm not interested."

"But everyone else is signing up!" (This last sentence spoken with a tone of incredulousness – the implication being that you are clearly one of the dumbest people on the planet).

You might respond with aggression and go one up (slamming down the phone,) passiveness (OK, I'll sign up,) or passive-aggressiveness (OK just hold on while I go get a pen – but then you leave the house for your three week vacation.)

What would be an assertive option in this situation? You have said no clearly and succinctly. You have reiterated your position. There can be no doubt as to your answer and yet the other person is not respecting that answer. You have given them the benefit of the doubt by being clear and concise and by restating your position, but they are not respecting your courtesy in return. What do you do now? How many times do you have to persist?

The Art of Persistence

Persistence means you may have to state your assertion at least twice. However, stating your position three times should be the maximum. There is no need to continue, as you have been exceedingly clear. More repetition is not the answer. So what do you do after you have said no two or three times?

First, take the issue of saying no off the table. That's done. You've made your position clear and there's no reason to belabour the point. Instead, the focus becomes about the other person's lack of respect for your answer. You confront that lack of respect and you hold them accountable for their actions:

"I have said no several times and yet you persist in asking me. That feels very disrespectful to me. Why are you not respecting my answer?"

"But everyone knows this is a great deal!"

"That's exactly what I mean. I see that you are again ignoring what I'm saying. I find that very disrespectful. Why are you doing that?"

"Look buddy, I'm just doing my job."

"Well, I would like you to respect my answer."

Another example:

"No, you can't borrow my car."

"Come on, it's just for a few hours."

"No."

"I'll fill it up this time!"

"No."

"It's not like you have a Caddy or something. It's just a piece of junk!"

"I've said no to you three times now and yet you keep asking anyway. I don't like that. I find what you are doing disrespectful and rude. Why are you doing that?"

"Gee, it's just an old clunker."

"Look at what you're doing. Why are you not taking no for an answer? What's going on?"

Instead of respecting your clear answer, the person escalates and insults your car. You respond by confronting the disrespect; that disregard now becomes the issue. The issue is the person's behaviour and your confrontation, in the spirit of Satyagraha, shines a light on their behaviour:

"Look at what you are doing. You're not respecting my answer."

Imagine a world where everyone held others accountable in an assertive and respectful way. Those disrespectful actions would become glaringly obvious in the illuminating light of assertion.

In assertiveness, you take responsibility for yourself. You stand up for your right to be treated with respect, while holding the other person accountable for their actions. You can't control what the other person does or how they respond to you. All you can do is take charge of how you handle the situation. Hopefully, the other person will respond to your assertion in a reasonable way, but you have no control over that; that's their stuff. Assertiveness is not about controlling other people. It's about how you live in your relationships.

Responding To A Passive-Aggressive Person

Another difficult assertive situation is responding to someone who is being passive-aggressive. This can be even more difficult than responding to aggression, because, unlike aggression, the meaning of the passive-aggressive behavior is veiled and hidden. In fact, the punitive intent of passive-aggression is often denied outright.

A colleague informed a manager that a meeting was being held without her knowledge:

"I think you need to come to this meeting because they're talking about you in there."

The manager entered the meeting room and was surprised to discover that not only was a meeting in progress but also that she was the focus of the meeting. Another co-worker had set up the meeting without advising her. The themes being discussed were a list of criticisms about how she was doing her job. She was the only one of her colleagues that had not been invited or informed of the meeting; it was all done behind her back.

The manager inquired as to who set up this meeting:

"I wasn't made aware of this meeting or the agenda. Who arranged for this meeting?"

The passive-aggressive co-worker responded:

"Well I'm glad you're finally here, you need to hear this."

"I find it very disrespectful that you called a meeting like this behind my back, without informing me. Also, it's actually our written policy that if you have a criticism or difficulty with someone, that you discuss it directly with them first. That's the respectful way of dealing with issues. This is the first I'm hearing of this and I think it would have been respectful to approach me first."

"Well, we're all here now so let's go over your performance problems."

"No. I won't participate in this type of meeting where my basic rights haven't been respected. Also, I don't want you to make any further critical comments about me to others behind my back. If you have an issue, come and see me directly."

The manager then walked out of the meeting. The meeting ended abruptly as others followed her lead. Co-workers approached the manager and told her that they had not been made aware that the meeting had been set up behind her back. They confided that they were embarrassed and angry at being put in the position of seeming to be a part of such unethical behavior.

The manager's assertive response to the passive-aggression had illuminated the disrespectful and inappropriateness of the actions for all to see. Her colleagues became wary of their passive-aggressive co-worker as a result. In contrast, the manager's assertive response was admired and respected by her fellow workers and her leadership qualities became very evident. She was promoted to a higher level in management, partly because of her demonstration of managing a difficult and passive-aggressive co-worker with firmness, dignity and respect.

Illuminating Passive-Aggressive Behavior

The assertive response to passive-aggression is to clearly name what is going on, in order to bring it out of the shadows. You call the person on their manipulation and this illuminates the issue. Bringing the issues out into the open then places accountability onto the person who is avoiding responsibility through their manipulation and indirection.

If you are repeatedly assertive, the passive-aggressive person quickly learns that they can no longer punish you from behind your back and that they will be called on their actions and held accountable. This leaves them with the options of either becoming more assertive themselves or to move on and seek easier targets for their ambushes.

JENNIFER'S TRANSFORMATION: PART II

Remember Jennifer's difficulty with the invasive co-worker? Her situation involved dealing with both passive-aggressive behavior and responding to someone who refused to take no for an answer. How did it turn out? Was assertiveness helpful?

Jennifer practiced an assertiveness role-play around this workplace issue. During the role-play, she became able to express herself clearly and to the point.

She was asked the question: what do you want in this situation? She identified her answer to that question, using an 'I' statement:

"I do not want to talk about personal issues at work."

She practiced sorting the issues during the role-play, as well as confronting disrespectful statements. She felt empowered and energized in the role-play and was even looking forward to the following Monday when she could confront the co-worker. The following week, I inquired as to how it had gone:

Dr. Welburn: "We worked on that role play of how you might set some limits with your co-worker who was invasive in asking you questions about your personal life."

Jennifer: "Yes, I told her I don't want to talk about personal life at work and she kept pushing it and I said: why can't you just respect me with these boundaries? She got pretty irate with me, actually. She said: I don't understand why you are making such a big deal of this. I'm just concerned for you.

I said: Well, to me it feels that you are being nosey and I don't want to get into it.

Then she went around and spoke to some of the other co-workers (behind Jennifer's back) and called me a few names and told people that I'm not approachable."

Dr. Welburn: "Passive-aggressive."

Jennifer: "Yeah and later that day somebody came up to me to ask me something and she said, very sarcastically: oh, don't talk to her, you are invading her personal space!"

Dr. Welburn: "So how did you handle that?"

Jennifer: "I just looked at her and said: I would like you to respect that I don't want to get into personal things with you. It has nothing to do with what's going on at work. Work related is one thing and personal life is another. I don't want to answer all your questions about my personal life."

Dr. Welburn: "So she was not letting it go but you persisted in being assertive."

Jennifer: "Yeah, but I told her again and I tried to stay calm."

Dr. Welburn: "How did it feel to do that?"

Jennifer: "Scary, but good. I'm not usually like that. I usually just bow my head and try to avoid everything. (She describes the posture of taking a one-down position in the relationship. The bowed head puts her into a dis-empowered and passive state.)

I was kind of scared but I remembered that, when we were doing the role-play last week, I had just felt so powerful inside."

Dr. Welburn: "That's terrific! You remembered the feeling of empowerment that you got in the role-play and that helped you to be assertive."

Jennifer: "Yes. And I've worked with her since and she seems to be fine now and she's no longer asking about my personal life."

Dr. Welburn: "That's a big change."

Jennifer: "I just don't think she was listening to the wording I was using. She took it as a personal attack and that was not what I was trying to do."

Dr. Welburn: "You persisted, during the interaction with her and also later on, when she made those sarcastic comments, you just stuck to your guns. You didn't escalate it either."

Jennifer: "Yeah and that was in front of a couple of other girls as well. She brought it up in front of other staff. But I just said this has nothing to do with work, it has to do with you coming to me for my personal information and I don't want to discuss it."

Dr. Welburn: "And that's her stuff, right? So, what you did is to take ownership for your stuff."

Jennifer: Yes and I feel a whole lot better about it."

Dr. Welburn: "That's great. So you didn't feel anxious? I remember that before you were even feeling afraid to go into work, anticipating it, full of anxiety?"

Jennifer: "Yes, because it's been building for so long and the situation's been going on for so long, ever since I got back to work. I was afraid to say the wrong thing, so I think that's why I beat around the bush with her."

Dr. Welburn: "Just how long has it been going on?"

Jennifer: "Almost a year! I feel like everyone was so curious as to what was going on in my personal life. I didn't want to bring my personal life into work and she couldn't accept that, but now I think she does."

Dr. Welburn: "I think it's because you were so clear and persistent and you didn't clobber her. You didn't go one-up and you didn't go one-down either, which is normally how you would respond. You said that you would often bow your head and take a one down position, right?"

Jennifer: "Yes, but this time I couldn't wait to do it! I even drove faster to get to work because I wanted to make sure I kept the confidence. I knew she would approach me. So it really helped when we did the role-play."

Dr. Welburn: "So the role-play first helped you by having the venue to practice saying the words."

Jennifer: "Yes and after that I just kept practicing so I would have the confidence for when I walked in to work, because I knew that as soon as she showed up, she'd be at me again."

Dr. Welburn. "Terrific, and today you look calmer and more confident in yourself."

Jennifer: "It helped a lot."

Dr. Welburn: "Has it changed how you feel, outside of that particular situation?" (It is not the specific incident that matters so much. She may win some and she may lose some, but what is important is that she is changing the patterns of how she responds to these situations. That's the emergence of social empowerment through assertiveness.)

Jennifer: "I feel calmer. She was the one I was always trying to avoid at work. Going into work and knowing she'd be staring at me, it would always bother me. But now, it's just like that whole – *well, bring it on* – attitude. Not to be mean or rude, I just have the confidence now that, if anyone approaches me, I know how to handle it."

Dr. Welburn: "Even when she was persistent and she came back to it, you still set a limit with her, but you kept it short, it didn't go on for that long."

Jennifer: "I didn't want to let it. I was afraid that when she started to bring it up again, that it would just keep going on, so I looked her straight in the eye. (She used congruent body language to underline her verbal message.) I said that what we discussed earlier was not work related and I said that in front of a group of co-workers. I don't know how that made her feel, but I know I felt fine."

Dr. Welburn: "Yeah, all you can do is treat her with respect and you were very firm about setting a very reasonable limit, which is, of course, your right. The other thing is that the co-workers see that too, as you were modeling personal empowerment. So the people who are referring to it as the same thing they get with her, now they have that model for how they might handle it."

Jennifer: "Yeah, it's good and I'm feeling so much more confident."

16
Embracing Conflict

"We have wars because we are so inept at having lesser conflicts."

CONFLICT

On a cold and remote mountain pass, at an altitude of 10,000 feet in the Otzal Alps, near the meeting place of the Austrian and Italian borders, hikers discovered an ice-bound mummy of a man from the Neolithic era. He came to be known as Ötzi, the ice-man. Ötzi's body was so well preserved that the hikers thought they had stumbled upon the corpse of a newly deceased mountaineer. Scientists later determined that Ötzi was actually 5300 years old, the oldest European mummy ever discovered.

His clothing was elaborate and intact and his time-capsuled body was accompanied across the great chasm of time by several curious artefacts: a copper axe, a knife and a quiver containing 14 arrows. The ice that encapsulated Ötzi and his belongings transmitted the story of his life and death across the millenniums. The melting of the ancient glacier had washed away the fog of the past to reveal an archetypal story of human violence and conflict. Scientists using forensic analysis from the 21st century determined that Ötzi had been shot in the left shoulder by an arrow. Ötzi had bruises and deep cuts on his hands and chest and cerebral trauma was evident on his head. There were traces of blood from four other people on his knife, arrows and coat. Data from an autopsy and analysis of the genetic material revealed a violent death after an ongoing struggle. He had retrieved and re-used his arrows from two different individuals that he had killed, only to be killed himself by an arrow shot at him from behind, followed by a blow to the head. Modern science paints a vivid picture of the ice-man's death and in doing so, tells an ancient and sadly familiar story of humans in violent conflict.

AN ASSERTIVE MODEL OF CONFLICT

The word conflict has a number of synonyms, including war and engagement. These two definitions give very different pictures of conflict. War is violent, bloody, deadly, destructive and traumatizing. War is resolved when one party dominates and the other submits.

CONFLICT AS ENGAGEMENT

Engagement is about people connecting with each other in an authentic, meaningful and passionate way. Engagement implies presence, interaction, commitment and activity. The engagement model of conflict fits well with assertiveness and social empowerment. In passiveness, you submit or avoid, in aggression, you dominate and belittle, but in assertiveness you engage with the other person. You encounter the other person in a committed, active and authentic way, even when there is some difference of opinion. The importance of an engagement model of conflict lies not in the resolution of the conflict but rather in what happens during the engagement itself.

In practicing assertiveness, it helps to develop a comfort level with conflict. It is necessary to embrace conflict rather than flee from it. Assertive conflict has a different quality and feel to it than aggression. Aggressive conflict is disrespectful in manner and escalating in process while assertively engaged conflict is neither. Assertive conflict maintains a respectful attitude towards the other person throughout the interaction while also maintaining your own integrity. It is mutually respectful.

Assertive conflict is non-escalating. You neither go one-up nor do you become submissive and assume a one-down position. You take responsibility for yourself while holding the other person accountable for their actions. You engage in the conflict in a real and authentic way, without dominating the other person.

CONFLICT AND ACCOUNTABILITY

Sometimes others let you down or treat you in a way that you find to be less than respectful. That means conflict: you want to be treated with respect and the other person is not doing so. In dealing with the conflict assertively, you engage the other person and hold them accountable for their actions.

A young mother was volunteering to help out with the management of her daughter's soccer team. At the start of the season she picked up the new soccer uniforms and arranged for the other parents to meet her in the soccer field so that she could distribute the uniforms. She waited with her daughter in the field with the box of uniforms but only a few parents showed up at the agreed upon time.

Client: Most of the parents never showed up, so I got out the list and I called every one of them. I said: I sent you an email, so why aren't you here? Everyone responded: oh something happened and one guy said he didn't want to come. I said that's up to you but then you'll have to make other arrangements. He ended up coming to pick up the uniform."

Dr. Welburn: "You literally called people on it."

Client: "Right there in the parking lot! I wasn't aggressive. One woman was sick so that's understandable and two of the people weren't getting the emails because they copied them down wrong. So, for the woman who was sick, I dropped it off for her on my way home."

Dr. Welburn: "So you just, spontaneously, from the field, picked up your cell phone and phoned all the people who weren't there to pick up the shirts for their kids."

Client: "Yes, and for the people that I left messages with I said: I hope nothing happened because I waited forty-five minutes. Please get back to me in terms of when you can make arrangement to do this."

Dr. Welburn: "You held everyone accountable. You put it back to them to now take responsibility for getting the uniform. What did that feel like?"

Client: "Awesome! This is *my* time, I'm giving up my time to volunteer and to help with soccer and with your children and you owe me the same respect."

Dr. Welburn: "Exactly. It's about that balance, where you're willing to give and help and those are wonderful traits, but you're also going to hold other people accountable, too, for how they treat you. You have value and you have the right to be treated with the same respect that you give anybody else."

Client: "Exactly, that's what I wanted to teach my daughter. She didn't want me to call anyone. She was horrified that I was going to call them but I said: no, we made an effort to be here and they said they were coming and I'm not waiting any longer than ten minutes."

Dr. Welburn: "Your daughter is saying: I think you should avoid the conflict, conflict is scary, so can't we just avoid it? And it would just be so easy to avoid it, but you are telling her: no, it's okay to have a conflict. It's not that dangerous. So you are teaching her something valuable. When you phoned them and then they showed up, you actually solved some problems because some weren't getting the emails, now they can. If you hadn't engaged in the conflict and spoke up, none of that would have gotten solved.

That's good modeling for your daughter, because you want her to learn to be comfortable having a conflict. Conflict is there everyday in life. When she's an adult and she goes to work and encounters a bully, you want her to be able to go: 'hey wait a minute, I don't like that,' and not spend months asking herself: 'Gee, did I do something wrong?"

In this moment in her life, this mother is confronted with a conflict. On a sunny Saturday afternoon, she stands in an empty soccer field, waiting for the parents to show up as they've agreed. She has followed through on her commitment but the others have not. She doesn't know why they are not there, but it feels disrespectful. Maybe it means that she is not worthy of respect. Maybe it means she is not as important as other people with their busy schedules. She is very good at following through on her commitments but she is less comfortable in asking others to do the same. What should she do next? Should she leave with her head hung low, avoid the anxiety of having to confront the missing parents and swallow the feelings of frustration and disrespect? If she does nothing, her avoidance will entrench any negative beliefs about herself such as: 'My time is not valuable.' 'I'm not valuable.' 'I don't deserve to be treated with respect.'

Happily, she decides to take action to confront the situation. From that small act of courage, the seeds of empowerment are born. She embraces the conflict, respectfully holds others accountable for their actions and is transformed in the process. Tackling the issue directly illuminates the conflict. It becomes apparent why the parents are missing. Her actions reinforce that she and her time are valuable and deserve respect. She teaches herself, her daughter and the missing parents that she has a right to be respected.

She learns that she is a good problem solver, that she can confront others to get at the truth of things and that it is possible for everyone to benefit from that process. She holds her head up high and her shoulders straighter in a posture of empowerment. Her daughter watches this happen, encoding this information in the deep recesses of her brain. Her daughter sees her mother being comfortable with the conflict. She sees that the conflict doesn't escalate and is respectful. She has observed a model for how to engage in conflict in a positive and helpful way and she now has an alternative to blindly following her instinct to just avoid the whole thing.

CONFLICT WITH AN AGGRESSIVE PERSON

How do you respond to a conflict where the other person is being abusive, intimidating or disrespectful? The assertive option is to focus immediately and solely on the aggression. Keep it brief and focused. The breach of respect becomes the single issue. Remember that it takes two to escalate and your power resides in maintaining an assertive stance: neither escalating nor assuming a one-down position. The aggressive person is actually seeking a passive or aggressive response, in order to bully or vent. They want you to cave in, thus establishing their dominance, or to get in a fight with you, so they can unleash their anger. Responding assertively encourages neither, while illuminating and highlighting the inappropriateness of their actions.

A nurse in a psychiatric hospital walked down a hallway, when a patient stopped her to ask for a cigarette:

"I don't have any."

"Well then, give me some money so I can buy some."

"No, but you can see patient services and ask them."

"I want it now! You stupid cow...." The patient then

launches into a loud, angry and abusive tirade involving curse words and putdowns.

The nurse felt shocked and afraid in the face of the sudden and unexpected angry outburst. She wondered if the patient would become physically violent. After a moment or two of silence, she recovered from her shock and made an assertive response:

"I find what you're saying to be very rude and offensive. I treated you with respect and now look what you're doing."

She didn't wait for an answer but instead abruptly turned and walked off down the hallway, not feeling safe until she had put some distance between her and the aggressive patient. She felt shaken by the interaction and had many emotions as a result, including fear, anger, helplessness and shock over the unexpectedness of the outburst. She also felt proud of standing up for herself in the face of the sudden aggression and in spite of the fear she felt in response to the verbal attack. She was glad that she had said what she did but also felt that she really hadn't had much impact on the situation. The patient had seemed oblivious to her comments. She was also fearful of what might happen in the future if she were to encounter the same patient. Would he be out to get her, now that she had stood up to him?

She got her answer two days later when she did run into the same man in another hallway. To her great surprise (and relief), he immediately apologized for his actions:

"Look, I'm really sorry about the way I talked to you the other day. I was having a really bad day. They're changing my meds. I know that's no excuse, but I was having an awful time and I'm not usually like that. You were right about everything you said – it was very disrespectful. I'm sorry."

The nurse accepted his apology and congratulated him on taking responsibility for himself. They were both smiling when they parted and her feelings of being unsafe dissipated. The feelings of fear, shock, helplessness and anger also faded, but the sense of being proud of herself for how she handled the situation grew stronger.

In the face of the unexpected aggressive attitude she had maintained an assertive response of mutual respect, taking neither a one-up nor a one-down position. She kept her response brief and precise and removed herself quickly from the physical space in an effort to make herself safe.

Should you always respond to aggression with assertion? How do you know if you will be safe if you do so? The answer, of course, is that you don't know with certainty the outcomes from your actions. There is an aspect of uncertainty in all of your interactions, no matter how cautious you might try to be. Every interaction has to be judged on its unique characteristics and the element of immediate safety should, of course, be a very important consideration. However, if you never respond to aggression with assertiveness the aggression grows unimpeded. If you never stand up to bullies, the bullying will escalate and the bullies of the world gain even more power over others.

Assertiveness, in the spirit of Satyagraha (truth-force), means that others are held accountable for their actions. That requires courage and involves taking some risks in an unpredictable world. It's a choice and comes with no guarantees of how the other person might respond.

Imagine a world where people would naturally stand up to aggression with assertion. How difficult would it be then for the aggressor to keep on that aggressive path? What if children were taught this, at a very young age, so that they developed a comfort level with responding to aggression with respectful assertion?

Avoidance of conflict at all costs is a pattern that results in an ongoing vulnerability to the bullies of the world. Ultimately, it manifests in more aggression, not less. We need to learn to be comfortable with conflict and to view it as part of the human condition. We have wars because we are so inept at having lesser conflicts.

17
Guilt, Anxiety and Negative Core Beliefs

"Put your own oxygen mask on first."

Airline safety instructions.

Y ou can fully understand the skills of assertiveness and yet continue to be passive in your relationships, in spite of that knowledge. You know what to do, but you don't actually follow through and do it. What's going on?

The usual suspects in this scenario are: guilt, anxiety and negative core beliefs. In fact this trio of dysfunction invariably go together. Guilt and anxiety are the emotional indication that some underlying negative and self-limiting core belief has been activated. Those negative core beliefs are like water flowing underground. You discover it's there only when something bubbles up to the surface. Exploring those moments of guilt and anxiety can be enlightening in an effort to discover what is stirring deep in your unconsciousness.

GUILT: WHAT IS IT GOOD FOR?

Guilt, like all human emotions, serves a valuable purpose. Guilt is the emotion that tells you that you are not living up to your internal code. Everyone has an internal set of rules that they try to live by. Guilt is the emotional flag that you are straying from the path of those rules. It's like having a little alarm bell that goes off to alert you to correct your course and get back on track. For example, let's say you have a rule: don't talk about your friends behind their back. Then, being all too human, you gossip about your friend. Violating your internal rule then results in feelings of guilt. As a result, you feel bad and you resolve to not gossip again. The guilt has served its purpose and steered you back onto the straight and narrow. You can start to feel good about yourself again.

However, sometimes you feel guilty but, on reflection, you can't see what it is that you have done wrong. This is all too common when you live with chronic guilt and anxiety. However, it may not be your *behavior* that needs to change, but rather the internal *rules* themselves that need some restructuring. The guilt is an indication of unreasonable, self-defeating rules (negative schema) that you learned and now are keeping you stuck in an unhealthy and dysfunctional pattern of passivity. Guilt doesn't discriminate reasonable rules from dysfunctional rules; it merely alerts you to the fact that you are breaking the rules.

DYSFUNCTIONAL RULES TO (NOT) LIVE BY

"I should always look after others."
"I should always keep busy."
"I should always be productive."
"Don't just sit around."
"Never fail."
"You should never put yourself first."

"Never argue with the teacher (or any authority figure)."

"Don't think of yourself."

"Don't upset anyone."

"I should always help out."

"Don't ask for anything."

"Always do your best at everything you do."

"Never let anyone down."

The implication in these all too common rules is that you should never say no to any request. Nor should you consider your own feelings above others or evaluate what it is that you want in the situation. Furthermore, you should always go along with authority in a blind, unquestioning fashion. Remember King Šuruppak's advice to his son Ziasudra: you should submit to the respected and you should be obedient to your elders? Notice the *should's,* dating back to the earliest writing of human civilization. It is evident in these writings that the ancient Sumerians were quite familiar with guilt and anxiety.

Some of these rules don't seem so unreasonable on first glance. Always do your best at everything you try seems like a good idea, but what is the value in applying your maximum effort and unrelenting perfectionism to all the things that you do during the day? It's an exhausting way to live.

Notice the extreme nature of these rules: always, never, should and so on. These injunctions lack balance and it is their unbending nature that makes them so dysfunctional. They are the very anti-thesis of personal empowerment. Instead, they lead you to powerlessness and to a denial of your true self.

THE SELF-PERPETUATING NATURE OF SCHEMAS

You encounter feelings of guilt when you begin to practice standing up for your self and expressing your thoughts and opinions. However, it is the dysfunctional rules that need to change and not your new and burgeoning attempts towards empowerment. The challenge is that schemas are self-perpetuating; they maintain themselves over time through multiple self-corrections arising from the emotional experience of guilt. Therefore, in order to change your core beliefs, it necessitates tolerating some guilt while persevering in the assertive behavior. If you travel to England from Canada and drive on the left side of the road, you will at first have a feeling that you are doing something wrong. However, if you persist in that behavior, the anxious feelings dissipate and the new rules thus become internalized. It is no different with social or self-esteem rules. Feel the guilt and do it anyway. It helps to remind yourself that the new way of doing things is actually good for you. Do that a hundred times.

EVOKING YOUR CORE BELIEFS

Emerging feelings of dysfunctional guilt signal the activation of an underlying schema. The good news is that when the core belief is active, possibilities for change are also present. You have to evoke the beliefs in order to change them (Welburn, Dagg, Coristine & Pontefract, 2000). Conversely, when the core belief is dormant, no change can occur. For example, if you avoid all relationships, your care-taking, self-sacrificing schemas don't get evoked and so you feel better. Unfortunately, when you eventually do get into another relationship, the old patterns re-emerge.

It is necessary to evoke the schema, tolerate some guilt, and do something different in the face of those emotions, in order to bring about change in the underlying core belief. You will need to challenge the guilt repeatedly in order to ultimately break free of that old dysfunctional pattern.

But what do I do with these guilt feelings when they come up? You can use guilt as the signal to practice coaching yourself with a new and healthier belief. This is an excellent place to practice all the elements of good coaching: use compassionate, positive and encouraging self-talk while breathing diaphragmatically. Good coaching will assist you in replacing the old dysfunctional rules with healthier and more balanced rules. Persistent coaching, while tolerating some guilt and persevering in your new way of doing things will hasten these changes.

You say no to some request and you feel guilty. You realize that you haven't really done anything wrong but that you have broken the rule: "Always look after others." You have identified a new belief: "Sometimes it's important to put myself first." The guilt becomes a cue to practice the new belief. You take a diaphragmatic breath and you say to yourself:

"Sometimes it's important to put myself first."

You repeat this several times. You use an encouraging, confident and compassionate tone of voice. You might paraphrase the new belief:

"I am taking care of myself and that's good."

"I really do need to look after myself.'

"I'm proud of me for saying no."

"It's good to respect myself."

Type the new belief into your cell phone or write it down on a card that you keep with you. Remember the game: whack-a-mole? Think of this as whack-the-guilt. Whenever the guilt pops up, whack it by immediately reading the card:

"It's good to respect myself."

Memorize the card so you can whack the guilt even faster. Do that whenever the guilt emerges but also start to say the new belief proactively, before the guilt pops up. Do that a hundred times and notice that you now have a new belief.

BALANCED RULES TO LIVE BY

"Sometimes it's important to put my self first."

"It is good to take time to play and not just work all the time."

"It's OK to do less than I am humanely capable of."

"You can't win them all. It's good to win some."

"Respect others, but also respect myself."

"It's good to tune in to my self and respect what's there."

"You can't please everyone and that's OK."

"Help out when it's reasonable to do so and let others help you as well."

"It's healthy to ask for what I need."

"It's important to listen to what feels right to me."

THE RELATIONSHIP BETWEEN ANXIETY AND ASSERTIVENESS

Guilt is the emotion that signals when you deviate from your internal code. What about anxiety? Is there some purpose to this unpleasant emotion as well? Can anxiety be helpful in some way?

As you've learned earlier, anxiety, in two words, is: Danger ➔ Escape. Let's take a minute to review so that the association between anxiety and assertiveness becomes clear. Anxiety exists in the fear continuum of emotion and alerts you when you are being faced with some danger or threat. Your conscious mind thinks 'danger' and, deep in the mid-brain, the amygdala rouses and responds to the message of threat by sending out a signal for increased arousal in order to run away (escape) from the danger. This means sympathetic nervous system arousal such as increased heart rate, rapid and shallow breathing, sweating in anticipation of heating up by running away from the danger and an infusion of adrenalin and glucose to provide extra energy in the service of escaping from the danger. Blood flow is rerouted away from the internal organs:

"Forget digesting your food, you've got to run!"

The change in blood flow may result in butterflies in the stomach, queasiness in the guts or even diarrhea.

These highly unpleasant symptoms are actually manifestations of an adaptive response of the body to the indication of the threat of some looming danger. Your body is simply trying to help you out and get you away from the danger. It's the fight or flight response, but anxiety is usually about the flight option. Increased arousal helps to speed your escape from the danger. The arousal means that you can run faster.

There doesn't actually have to be a real, external danger for this response to occur, all that's required is that your mind calls out the DANGER! alarm. You approach some situation, your DANGER! alarm gets activated and you make a quick U-turn to get away from the perceived threat. Escaping then transforms into *avoidance* of the previously designated danger, as it is much more adaptive to just not go into the place of danger in the first place. Avoiding is better than fleeing. Danger ➜ Escape, thus becomes: Danger ➜ Avoid. No U turns are required as you give the threatening situations a wide berth.

The reduction in anxiety that accompanies the avoidance feels like a huge relief and therefore reinforces your avoidant behavior. Your avoidance becomes even more entrenched. The avoidance generalizes as you now start avoiding other situations that you see as similar. Your world shrinks.

Here is the connection: passivity is a form of avoidance. Avoidance is the behavior of anxiety. Thus, passivity and anxiety are intrinsically connected. They go hand in hand. Not standing up for yourself, avoiding conflict at all costs and not stating your opinion are all forms of avoidance. It means that, on a cognitive level, you are evaluating those situations as inherently dangerous and threatening. Your passivity is a way of retreating from those threats and your passivity keeps you stuck in patterns of disempowerment.

ANXIETY AND NEGATIVE CORE BELIEFS

Negative core beliefs get in the way of learning assertiveness. Two ubiquitous negative core beliefs that are associated with anxiety and passivity are:

"The world is a dangerous place," and:

"I am incompetent in dealing with it."

These two generalized beliefs – *dangerous world* and *incompetent self* – become activated when you try to be assertive. They can keep you stuck in your passivity. These negative core beliefs are barriers to being more assertive in your relationships, even when you've learned assertiveness skills. You know what to do, but you don't do it. You stay passive.

In overcoming these barriers, it is helpful to identify exactly what it is that you are evaluating as dangerous. Confronting a situation that you have been avoiding will evoke the underlying belief. That's helpful because then you can identify it. Learning the exact nature of your core beliefs is the first step in changing them.

CATASTROPHIC EXPECTATIONS

"If I speak up, he'll leave me."

"If I say anything they'll get really mad."

"I'll be fired if I don't work late."

"She will hate me if I say no."

"They'll never talk to me again if I don't do what they want."

"I will fail if I'm not fully prepared for every possible outcome."

"I need to foresee anything that can go wrong."

These are examples of danger thoughts: extreme and catastrophic expectations about what will happen should you choose to be assertive. If these predictions were accurate, it would indeed make sense to avoid being assertive. However, these beliefs are usually in reaction to some past situation and may be less relevant to the present state of affairs. If you have catastrophic expectations, it is likely because you experienced catastrophic fallout at some time in your past. Through your experience, you learned that the world is a dangerous place. Now you continue to expect the bad stuff to happen again.

The present reality is that you are no longer in that situation yet you live as if you were still mired in the past chaos. You act is if you are in danger when in fact you are safe. Beliefs in a dangerous world don't go away easily just because you are out of the danger. Those beliefs were helpful and adaptive; they made you vigilant to threat in a dangerous world. Because they kept you safe, they are quite resistant to change. It's the same reason soldiers find it hard to adapt to home life after being in a war zone.

You have to work systematically to alter these beliefs. That requires making a number of acts of courage where you feel anxious, but you confront the situation anyway. The persistence and repetition of confronting the feared situations will alleviate the anxiety and challenge the catastrophic expectations. As you continue to be assertive, you learn that the world is not as dangerous as it once was, and yes, you can be effective in dealing with things. These are two new core beliefs. As you practice assertiveness, you enhance your sense of self-efficacy and competence. This, in turn, leads to more assertive behavior. You begin to feel comfortable with your newfound ability to stand up for your self; you develop mastery.

Unrealistic feelings of guilt and anxiety result in a vulnerability to manipulation and control by others and leave you with a sense of powerlessness. Revising self-limiting core beliefs enhances your sense of empowerment. Repeated assertion strengthens the sense of your competency and ability to cope with challenges in life, as you observe yourself being effective and having an impact on others.

A woman in her thirties, with two young children, was annoyed that her mother-in-law would frequently drop by unannounced. She experienced these visits as highly intrusive. She felt that she had to entertain her mother-in-law, while also trying to take care of her children and do the house cleaning and cooking. Her resentment towards her mother-in-law grew deeper with every visit.

She didn't express any of these resentments because she expected that her mother-in-law would then no longer talk to her. She would be abandoned. Worse, it would cause a conflict between her and her husband and the mother-in-law would turn him against her. She anticipated these extreme and catastrophic outcomes from being assertive. This is her version of:

"It's a dangerous world."

During assertiveness training she practiced confronting her mother-in-law by role-playing the situation. She rehearsed assertive responses that respected both herself and her mother-in-law. Then, in an act of courage, she followed through and tried out her assertive skills with her mother-in-law. This went much better than she had anticipated. Her mother-in-law was very understanding and hadn't realized that she was causing her daughter-in-law any stress. From her perspective, she had been investing her time in order to get to know her daughter-in-law, in an effort to build a relationship with her.

Now that things were out in the open, they scheduled times to get together that were more convenient for the daughter-in-law. Their relationship improved dramatically and the mother-in-law offered to babysit at times, in order to give her daughter-in-law a break from child rearing. This offer was happily accepted. The mother-in-law was now perceived as helping to lighten the load rather than adding to it. Resentments dissipated. She became closer to her mother-in-law and no longer viewed her as invasive, but rather as supportive.

Her belief in a dangerous world was challenged by these experiences. Her sense of self-efficacy and mastery was enhanced by her assertiveness and a new belief was reinforced:

"I can deal with things, after all."

18
Empowerment and Disempowerment

"Society is the sworn enemy of mental health."

Andrew Salter

PATTERNS OF DISEMPOWERMENT

In society, we teach patterns that inhibit empowerment. Many of these patterns were identified in the earliest writings on assertiveness (Salter, 1949) and remain pervasive in the modern world. These patterns are essentially recipes for powerlessness, anxiety and depression.

THE NEGATIVE LIST IS THIS:

1. Self-sacrificing
2. Care-taking others
3. People-pleasing
4. Unrelenting perfectionism
5. Obedience to authority
6. Avoiding conflict

These self-negating patterns create a vulnerability in the self that manifests in social issues such as bullying, harassment and violence in schools, the workplace and in the home. These dysfunctional patterns are elements in the present pandemic of depression and anxiety in society. Unable to satisfy the needs of others, failing to avoid every possible conflict, forever falling short of perfection, we spin into a vortex of helplessness, despair and fear.

The trans-generational reiteration of these patterns is the mechanism through which we become dissociated from our selves. The integrity and intentionality of the self have been lost, sacrificed on the altars of people-pleasing and conflict avoidance (Milgram, 1975; Zimbardo, 2007). The consequences are catastrophic; feelings of powerlessness, meaninglessness and alienation erupt into the world in devastating ways.

The negative list: self-sacrificing; care-taking; people-pleasing; perfectionism; obedience to authority; and avoiding conflict at all costs, represent different facets of the same underlying problem. The focus is on the other, rather than on tuning in to the self. The goal is to make someone else happy or to avoid someone else becoming upset rather than to consider your own needs and wants. The other is elevated and the self is diminished. The motivations driving these self-negating patterns are fear of rejection and the need for approval by others. Fear and neediness result in disempowerment.

SELF-SACRIFICE

Just about anywhere in the world you go, you can find a church. If you enter that church you will most likely be confronted with a startling but familiar image. The archetypal portrayal of Christ, nailed to the cross, dying, bloodied and in pain greets you with the exalted message of self-sacrifice.

It seems that it's Christ's death that matters, not his life. The greatest gift of all, you are told, is to sacrifice yourself for others. Guilt, anxiety and fear are the inevitable results of this disturbing but profoundly pervasive philosophy.

Imagine a parallel world where it was Christ's life that was iconic, rather than his death. In that world, the archetypal images would be of Christ laughing, dancing, carrying children on his shoulders, helping the poor and the sick, going up into the mountains for a well needed rest, even Christ the warrior overturning the tables of the money lenders.

These images portray vitality, strength, engagement and compassion. In that parallel world, using your skills to help others and standing up for what you believe to be right would be the exemplars for how to be in the world. Joy, courage, compassion and confidence in your self would be the accompanying emotional states rather than guilt, anxiety and fear.

CARE-TAKING OTHERS

Closely linked with self-sacrifice is the value of taking care of others. This value extolls the virtues of sacrificing your own needs in order to take care of someone else. It is as though you are being a good person only when you put others ahead of yourself; to do otherwise is selfish and shameful. The balance between the importance of your needs and the needs of the other becomes slanted in the favour of the other. If you try to consider your own needs, you feel guilty because you are breaking the rule that says: always put others first.

In care-taking, it is all too easy to assume misdirected responsibility for the other person. Their stuff becomes more important than your stuff. It's as if you have been elected to be in charge of someone else's life, thus diminishing their personal responsibility. You offer solutions and fixes, without being asked to do so, in an effort to be helpful. This behaviour presumes that they are inept in handling their own affairs. Care-taking can foster dependency on the part of the other person and reinforce any pre-existing core beliefs of incompetence. Care-taking interferes with self-responsibility.

PEOPLE-PLEASING

Every child strives to feel worthwhile. However, self-esteem is birthed from other-esteem. If you, as a child, are fortunate enough to receive sufficient esteem from your care-givers, you internalize it and this becomes the foundation for your self-esteem. However, if the world of your childhood is lacking in other-esteem, a feeling of never being good enough becomes internalized instead. You feel less than perfect and you strive to improve the situation by being a better little girl or boy.

You begin to feel that – no matter how much you try – you are just not good enough. Later in life, lacking the foundational core of self-esteem, you try to remedy the situation by seeking approval from others. That is the raison d'être for people-pleasing.

You put aside your own wants and desires in an effort to please others. The focus of your attention becomes fixated out there, on what others might want or expect of you. Because of that external focus, you become a stranger to yourself; you depersonalize and become less of the person that you truly are. Over time, your ability to tune in to your self becomes a forgotten art and you lose the connection with your deepest source of intentionality.

UNRELENTING PERFECTIONISM

Unrelenting perfectionism has the goal of achieving self-esteem through seeking and winning the approval of others. Dysfunctional perfectionism is not about quality improvement; instead, it has the aim of overcoming the deprivations and inadequacies of childhood. It emerges from a feeling of never quite being good enough.

You arrive proudly at home with ninety-nine per cent, only to be asked the foolish and damaging question of how you failed to obtain the missing one percent. Your real achievements are overlooked in a futile comparison with some impossible and absurd standard. Your sense of self is undermined. With the logic of a child, you imagine that if you only try harder you will eventually get it right and succeed in winning the approval you naturally seek as a child. You make a vow to try harder in everything you do and you persist in that effort into adulthood. Unfortunately, unrelenting perfectionism is doomed to failure; the past is done. The drive for perfection in order to gain the approval of others is actually counter-productive, as striving for unattainable perfection derails you from developing genuine self-esteem in the present.

OBEDIENCE TO AUTHORITY

Obedience to authority is yet another manifestation of people-pleasing. In your attempts to please others, you go along with the commands of those in power. Keeping the other person happy thus over-rides any sense of personal responsibility in the matter and your efforts to please others mean that you disregard your own moral code. "I was just following orders" becomes both an explanation and a justification for your actions. To the extent that you were following orders well, you might even view your actions as praise-worthy.

Obedience to authority is valued over having the courage of your convictions. This starts at a young age. The 'terrible twos' are named so because the child exhibits verbal disobedience to authority. It is that very defiance that is defined as terrible. Compliance is valued over will in the demanding world of the busy parent. The schedule of the parent clashes with the developmental needs of the child as the two-year-old attempts to experience empowerment, to disagree, to have her own idea about what should happen next and to express her intention. The exhausted parent is trying to make things move along within the limited demands of the day. How the parent and the two-year old engage in that conflict will have consequences that reverberate throughout the child's life. The worst possible, yet all too frequent outcome is that the child becomes adept at people-pleasing while learning to avoid conflict at all costs.

AVOIDING CONFLICT

Not surprisingly, children are encouraged to get along with others. This is especially true for females. "She plays well with others" is expressed as a compliment to which you as a parent can breathe a huge sigh of relief. It means that she will fit in. She will be accepted rather than rejected and you remember only too well those lingering pains of childhood rejection and exclusion. Maybe your daughter will escape that torture. Who wouldn't want such a thing?

The result, though, is that conflict becomes something to be avoided rather than mastered. The behavioural patterns instrumental in conflict avoidance are: people-pleasing, self-sacrificing, conforming, looking after others and trying even harder to be perfect. These are the seeds of disempowerment.

Fully engaging in conflict with others is avoided at all costs. From the ancient Sumerian civilization to the present day, children are exhorted to submit to those in authority, be humble in the presence of the powerful and to give obedience to those who are counted as superiors. The art and skill of conflict engagement is lost as a result.

A PARADIGM SHIFT

Bringing about a change in these tenacious and self-limiting patterns requires a change in the present view of power. Empowerment, meaning and connection must be central to the solution when powerlessness, meaninglessness and alienation are the forces that drive the problem. This requires a paradigm shift in the values and skills we teach to the next generation. The alternative is to stay the course for the next hundred years, thus maintaining the chronic situation where, as Andrew Salter (1949) notes: "society is the sworn enemy of mental health."

A society that genuinely fosters empowerment will not be the sworn enemy of mental health, but will instead become the healthy ground from which each individual can achieve his or her maximum potential. The creative expression of individuals within an empowering society then becomes the true wealth of the nation.

ALTERNATIVES TO DISEMPOWERMENT

If those six dysfunctional patterns represent the problem, what are the solutions? What would be healthier patterns associated with better mental health and greater quality of life?

DON'T SACRIFICE YOURSELF FOR OTHERS, ACTUALIZE YOURSELF FOR OTHERS

Self-sacrificing and care-taking others at the expense of one's own health are dysfunctional patterns that add to the ever growing mental health costs in society. Those patterns also result in a loss of creativity and productivity by the individuals within the society.

If you don't take care of yourself first, you deplete the resources you need to take care of anyone else. The airline safety instructions wisely advise you to "put your own oxygen mask on first".

When you model a self-depleting attitude to your children you train the next generation in the same self-negating behaviors, thus perpetuating the social pandemic of powerlessness, anxiety and depression.

The self needs not be sacrificed on the altar of doing for others. The more you tune into your self and respond to your own needs, the more you have to offer to the community. In the dialectic between the self and the community, it is the actualization of the individual that strengthens the community. The full actualization of the individual will manifest in artistic, economic and social enhancement of the society.

So, don't *sacrifice* yourself for others, *actualize* yourself for others. In other words, actualize your skills and capabilities and those talents will become your contribution to others. Think of your talents as gifts. Think of yourself as a gift. To paraphrase Ghandi: "Be the gift that you are to the world."

TAKE CARE OF YOUR SELF FIRST

In a healthy society there is a balance between the development of the individual and the enrichment of the community rather than favoring one at the expense of the other. I propose that a healthy balance is one in which the self is fifty-one percent important while the community is forty-nine percent important. The self needs to come first, but not extremely so, and the community needs to come a close second. This represents a healthy balance between the self and the community. The self is not diminished and giving back to the community remains an important value.

TUNE IN TO AND RESPECT YOURSELF

When you are driven by the need to please others, your focus and attention turn away from yourself and on to the other person. You lose touch with your self as a result, perhaps even losing your sense of identity. Tuning in to your self and then respecting what you discover, leads to a more integrated sense of identity. That, in turn, makes you less susceptible to the influence of others and more able to be internally directed. You act from yourself instead of reacting to the demands of the external world. That's the self-directed nature of empowerment.

USE PERFECT AS AN EXEMPLAR FOR PERSONAL GROWTH

A new, more useful paradigm for perfectionism is one based on success rather than on failure, and on building self-esteem rather than in fruitlessly seeking the approval of others. In order to establish a solid core of self-esteem it is essential to acknowledge and integrate one's achievements.

The concept of perfect can be used as a tool to successively improve your performance. It helps to set the bar somewhere so that you have something specific to aim for when you are learning a new skill. It is also necessary to recognize your improvements in working towards that ideal. That acknowledgement will build confidence and further hone your abilities.

Think of perfectionism as a peak performance skill. You visualize what the perfect outcome might be *before* the challenge at hand takes place. You create a model to which you can then aspire. This strategy gives you a perspective: what do you imagine that *perfect* would look like in this case? If you were to succeed in the challenge, what exactly would that look like? Then, because you have pre-established an exemplar of success, you have something to aim for, during the execution of the task. Afterwards, you can compare how you actually did against that image. You will be able to see how well you actually did and what could be improved in order to have an even better performance the next time. This will help fine-tune your performance in a succession of improvements leading towards the ideal. Instead of noticing how you are falling short, you notice how you are improving. It's success based rather than failure based.

OBEDIENCE TO YOUR SELF: INNER RULES

Rather than teaching obedience to authority, teach obedience to one's self. From that paradigm, it becomes important to help your children elaborate a system of values and ethics. It is likely that most parents would be hard pressed to identify their children's code of ethics and values. What are the rules you live by?

Presently, parents teach their children a set of values though the process of modeling. Much of the transmission of the parents value system happens without discussion or articulation. Children see how their parents act and imitate what they see, without debate. This learning is mostly unconscious and unspoken.

A new paradigm might involve parents making up a top ten list of rules to live by. The task would require a clear and conscious articulation of a value system. The resulting list would then be posted so that it is visible for all to see. The entire family could then be accountable to live up to the rules. Rules found to be extreme or unhealthy could be modified through discussion and engagement of the whole family.

EMBRACE CONFLICT

Rather than avoidance of conflict at all cost, it is helpful to teach children how to have a conflict. Conflict is an unavoidable and natural part of daily living. Learning how to comfortably engage in a conflict is an essential and empowering life tool.

Imagine a world where everyone possesses the skills to comfortably engage in conflict; it would surely be a very different place from the present world. We have wars because we are so inept at having lesser conflicts. Can you think of any more dysfunctional way of having a conflict than going to war?

We have been taught to avoid conflict so that when we finally do engage in one, it tends to be extreme. We need to get good at having smaller conflicts and we need to learn this early on in life, starting from the first moments we say no to something we don't want. Those moments are just as important as a child's first steps in that they represent the first steps towards empowerment.

SUMMARY OF GUIDELINES THAT PROMOTE EMPOWERMENT

1. Actualize yourself for others, don't sacrifice yourself for others.

2. Be the gift that you are to the world.

3. Care-take yourself, tune in to, honor and respect that self.

4. It's important to put yourself at least slightly first (51%) or you won't be healthy and helpful to others.

5. Be perfectionistic only when it matters. Remind yourself that you are valuable and worthwhile as a human being even when you are not perfect. Practice the skill of acknowledging what you do well while being able to set the bar to improve even more. Use perfect as an exemplar to grow and develop by visualizing the successful outcomes that you want to achieve before engaging in the task.

6. Practice obedience to yourself; develop a value system that guides you in the face of external pressures.

7. Learn to be comfortable engaging in conflict. It's a natural part of life. Practice having mutually respectful, non-escalating conflict. Take responsibility for yourself and hold others accountable for their actions. Embrace conflict instead of avoiding it.

19
Empowered Parenting

"You never parent the same child twice."

OBEDIENCE AND CONFORMITY

A young mother was excited to send her daughter, Mary, off to her first day at kindergarten. Mary was an exceptionally well-behaved and polite girl and she seemed to adapt to school easily, making friends and enjoying learning. Mary reported that she liked her school and that she was especially fond of her teacher. After a few weeks, the mother went in to meet the teacher at a parent-teacher get together.

"I'm so glad you're teaching Mary, she really likes you."

"Mary? I don't have a Mary in my class. You must have the wrong classroom."

"What? No, she mentioned you specifically. I don't understand."

The mother and teacher searched through the children's drawings until the mother pointed out her child's work.

"There, that's Mary's drawing right there! She *is* in your class."

"That's not Mary. That's Karen. At least that's what she has been calling herself."

Confused and troubled by this turn of events, the mother returned home and confronted her daughter.

"Mary, I don't understand, why have you been calling yourself Karen at school?"

Mary looked down at her feet.

"Well, mom, on the first day of school, the teacher was taking attendance and she looked at me and said: Karen? So I said: yes."

"Why on earth would you do that?"

Mary looked up at her mom with big eyes.

"Cause, mom, you said: never argue with the teacher!"

Parents teach obedience and conformity to children who are seeking their approval and so keenly absorb that teaching. Obedient children then go on to become obedient adults. The values of obedience and submission are taught while the value of empowerment is overlooked. Getting along is given more importance than having a voice.

Of course you do want your kids to be co-operative for the sake of expedience. The day-to-day challenges of parenting can result in moments of feeling powerless, frustrated and overwhelmed. More and more, families are composed of two working people trying to balance the time demands of raising children while simultaneously pursuing careers. Single parenting has also become more of a norm and the single parent is thus on call 24/7 with no one to share the load and allow for a needed break from the never-ending child-rearing tasks. It is not surprising that submission and compliance are taught as values. However, obedience is not distinguished from co-operation as a value. Obedience promotes being one-down in a relationship, whereas co-operation promotes equality and mutual respect.

EMPOWERED PARENTING

This chapter presents a model for empowered parenting. This parenting model is based on the platform of assertive empowerment and incorporates the philosophical principles and values previously outlined. Empowered parenting is an extension of personal empowerment.

Parenting is a complex, challenging and continuously shifting experience. In order to keep up to these changes, it seems you must always be re-inventing what you do as a parent. Children grow rapidly and are seemingly in a constant state of change and development. Like the adage that you never step into the same river twice, you never parent the same child twice. In empowered parenting, there are a few basic skills that will help to empower you and your child throughout the course of your child's evolution and your corresponding development as a parent.

The core empowered parenting skills remain the same regardless of your child's age. Implementing these skills will require creativity, planning and persistence. Empowered parenting is proactive, not reactive and therefore requires, forethought and analysis.

These parenting skills are certainly not meant to be everything that you need to be a parent. Rather, these skills represent some fundamental ways of being with your child that will be helpful and illuminating in facing the challenges of parenting over the years.

EMPOWERED PARENTING AND THE ART OF ATTUNEMENT

The fundamental skill of empowered parenting is attunement. In order to fully comprehend the challenges that your child is trying to manage, you first must tune in to your child. This needs to happen on a daily basis and become an ongoing part of your relationship with your child. It is a way-of-being-in-the-world with your child. It is this proactive, attuned connection that makes your child's developmental challenges accessible to you as a parent.

Tuning in to your child has two aspects: physical connection and empathic reflection. For example, when your child comes running up to you to show you his latest discovery or artwork, take a moment to give him your complete and undivided attention. Include a physical component, for example, by placing your hand on his back while you are speaking with him. Be fully present. Tune in to your child so that you can identify his emotional state. Use empathic reflection to verbalize your child's emotion in a way that that he will understand. In other words, say what you think your child is feeling:

"You are very excited about that robot!"

"You are proud of the picture you drew."

"You are angry at your brother for not sharing the toys."

If the empathic reflection is correct, your child will open up more as he feels understood. You get immediate feedback to your attempts in attuning to your child.

Attunement, as a way of being with your child, means that you take the time to have daily moments where you are fully present and available. For the most part, when a child wants your attention, they need it only briefly. Children have short attention spans and are soon off to seek new adventures. They are persistent only when they haven't experienced your presence enough and have become thirsty for connection with you. It is your full presence and engagement that satisfies the thirst of your child. In empowered parenting, you proactively let your child drink from your presence, on a daily basis, *before* they become thirsty. It's not about the activity; it's about presence and engagement.

Tuning in to your child leads to your child's ability to be able to tune in to herself. Your attention tells her that she matters and that how she is feeling is important. She is valuable. Over time, she internalizes your repeated engagement and develops the ability to identify her own wants, needs and emotional states. The newfound ability to tune in to herself represents the emergence of personal empowerment.

SEPARATION ANXIETY AND ATTUNEMENT

The following example illustrates the importance of repeated attunement in empowered parenting.

A thirty-four-year-old, single mother of a three-year-old, felt helpless in the face of her daughter's separation anxiety. Her daughter would scream and cry uncontrollably whenever being dropped off at daycare. The daughter would become inconsolable and the mother reacted by feeling overwhelmed and guilty at having to leave her daughter at the daycare in that state. She started to take days off of work to stay home with her daughter, but even that failed to mollify the young girl and she would again throw a tantrum upon returning to the daycare. The mother was extremely distressed by her daughter's emotional outbursts and felt guilty and embarrassed. She worried that she was not a good mother, but didn't know what to change.

She indicated that she spent daily time with her daughter and that they would in fact do many activities together. She was puzzled by her daughter's behaviour; nothing she tried seemed to work. She felt at her wit's end.

I encouraged the mother to practice tuning in to her daughter every day as the foundational skill for empowered parenting. She was to touch her child's arm or to be knee to knee while she tuned in to her daughter. She could do this in response to her daughter's requests, but she would also initiate some of these moments, proactively, on a daily basis. I suggested that she practice attunement several times a day, if only for a few moments each time:

"Your presence and engagement are so important and it doesn't have to be for a long time. It's can be just these brief moments. Even if there are two or three minutes where she is going: 'mommy mommy' – what she needs is to absorb you in that moment and so you can take thirty seconds or a minute to just be really present with her. Instead, if you are more concerned with keeping the order of the house and 'get in bed, it's past your bed-time, get in there now' – then she goes away frustrated. Then she comes back because she is still frustrated. It's as if she is thirsty and you have to give her another glass of water, but the glass of water is your presence and engagement. So just take a minute and give her your full attention and tune into her. You can touch her arm while you are doing that; give her that physical part too. You don't have to be there for the next two hours, and you don't have to feel that: now I can't do anything for myself."

The mother practiced having these moments of engagement over the following week. The experience turned out to be quite revealing. She discovered that she had been feeling overwhelmed with the thought:

"I am all alone and so it's entirely up to me to look after her for the rest of my life."

She, of course, felt enormous stress and anxiety whenever she had this thought. Her needs would forever be on the back burner and, to make matters worse, there would be no help forthcoming from anyone, ever. She had come out of a deprived childhood and that was the source of her anxiety-provoking thoughts. She had felt, as a child, that it was entirely up to her to look after herself and, in fact, that had been her experience. Her catastrophic beliefs were not arising from a failure of logic, but faithfully described the state of affairs that existed in her childhood. The young mother knew all too well what it was like to have her needs overlooked.

She had developed a distraction strategy in an effort to avoid these thoughts and reduce the accompanying anxiety. This strategy involved keeping busy at all times, particularly in those situations where the thought was most likely to arise:

when she was alone with her daughter. This helped her to avoid the emotional fallout from thinking about her enormous, relentless and inescapable responsibility. She would do many things with her daughter while not being truly present. Instead, she used the activity as a distraction and avoided tuning in to the three-year old, as she would then be confronted with her heavy responsibility and her aloneness. She engaged in the activity but not in the daughter.

In our previous session, I had asked her to visualize being connected and engaged with her daughter and having fun in the process. She was successfully able to imagine herself in the future, playing with her daughter and being fully present.

In the following session, I asked her if using the imagery had impacted on her experiences with her daughter:

Dr. Welburn: "I was wondering how it was going with your daughter, because she was having severe separation anxiety when you dropped her off at the daycare. Last time you were practicing imagery of being fully present and engaged with her. How is it going with her this week?"

Client: "It's going much better, I'm spending a lot more time being present in moments with her, and every day I make sure to do something, whether its twenty minutes or a couple of hours, it's something. I take her down to the river and we throw rocks. I play with her in the sand box. Sometimes we just lie in bed and look into each other's faces and talk. So I spend a lot of time just cuddling and looking at her, getting low and looking at her face. When I'm driving the car, I'll talk to her and that kind of thing. So I feel I'm doing a lot more of being present with her."

Dr. Welburn: "That's a big change. You're not distracting yourself like you were before."

Client: "It is good and I feel our connection is stronger and happier and she is doing a lot better with her anxiety. She is doing perfect at daycare, like in the morning when we get ready for day care."

Dr. Welburn: "That's huge, that's night and day from last week! Before, she was screaming and crying every time when you left. She had a very hard time."

Client: "Things are going better with my attending to her, calming her down, I'm touching her and my mood is better too. I am not as irritable as I used to be, so now, when I go in, I can attend to her. If she has to go to the washroom, I pick her up and carry her there. Bedtime routine is going much better too. I think everything is going better. It's so much easier now, but I have to work at it."

Dr. Welburn: "Yes, it is work to parent proactively. It does get easier as it becomes routine over time. Before, you were running all the time even when you were with her. It was a way of distracting yourself from your anxiety and that was getting in the way of you being present. So, when you are present now, what happens for you?"

Client: "Well when I am present, it's hard. It's like mindfulness where it's hard to be mindful all the time. I feel that way with her too, every single day around three, I get the anxiety. I have to go home now. What am I going to do tonight? I have to see her again, the full-timeness of it all sinks in and I get a bit of aloneness. But when I pick her up and we do something fun, we're just together and I'm being present and I enjoy it. I don't have the anxiety because I get caught up in the fun. It's all going so much better."

Dr. Welburn: "You need to tune in to yourself as well. It's parallel with what you do for her. You tune into her and say: what do you need right now? Remember, she often doesn't even know what she needs. Maybe she needs to connect with you so you can ask: "How do you feel, sweetie?" You can put your arm around her give her a kiss and then she goes to bed. That's what she needs.

You need to do the same thing for yourself, to tune into yourself and say – what do I need? As a parent, you can't just give all of the time. You have to preserve and nourish yourself. You didn't get, in your childhood, what you are giving her. It sounds like you are on the path to doing that now because some of those activities we discussed earlier, like the dancing and the exercise. You are starting to tune in to yourself and respect what you need as well."

Client: "I do need to find ways to continue to fit my needs in. I think I'm doing okay; I'm still breathing and adjusting. I just need to continue that so I find balance."

IDENTIFYING THE DEVELOPMENTAL CHALLENGE

Assertiveness starts with the question:

"What do I want in this particular situation?"

Empowered parenting starts with the question:

"What is my child trying to master in this situation?"

Empowered parenting requires that you make a thoughtful analysis of the specific developmental task that your child is currently facing. In other words, what is it that your child is trying to master? That is the fundamental starting point for empowered parenting. The empowered parent thinks before acting and comes up with a plan.

Once you have identified the challenge that your child is trying to master, you become vigilant in looking for opportunities where you can help your child to master that challenge. As an empowered parent you don't carry out the task for your child, but you do facilitate your child in developing mastery.

There has been a recent movement in the school system to not expect anything from the child. Everyone gets an award regardless of effort or outcome. You pass an assignment even though you didn't hand in any work. These strategies will not result in empowerment. Instead, they lead to a sense of entitlement, as if you somehow deserve results without making any effort. This teaching method means you are not being well prepared for facing challenges in life; you don't learn how to strive, how to face challenges and therefore you are unable to develop a sense of mastery. Only striving results in mastery. In empowered parenting, you don't face the challenge for your child, instead you help the child rise to the occasion and master the challenge.

Empowered parenting results in you having greater impact on the growth and development of your child. At the same time, it's about empowering your child to grow and develop in ways that encourage mastery, competence and confidence. The results are that both parent and child become empowered.

PROACTIVE VS. REACTIVE PARENTING

Empowered parenting is proactive rather than reactive. Empowered parenting means that you practice tuning in to your child everyday. You make physical contact and you empathically reflect what your child is feeling, on a daily basis. What you are doing here is laying the groundwork, so that you have the tools to manage the more difficult parts of parenting when they can and do emerge in the future. You build that connection before the challenges arise.

In contrast, reactive parenting springs from your emotional responses to your child's immediate actions in the present. The goal of reactive parenting is aimed at controlling the situation or the child's behaviour, in some way that will ultimately benefit you, the parent. You, not unreasonably, would like some peace and quiet or not to have to do so much housework:

"Don't be so loud."

"I told you to make your bed. "

"You're making such a mess! How many times have I told you to put your clothes away?"

Reacting to the child's behavior has the goal of making yourself feel better in some way: for example, the child is quieter so your headache doesn't get worse. Reactive parenting has the goal of returning to a previous state – achieving homeostasis. You get away from your bad feelings and return to your previous, calmer state. In contrast, proactive responding has the goals of growth and movement towards something new. Empowered parenting appreciates the reality that you never parent the same child twice. Proactive parenting helps your child attain the next step in their development.

THE TERRIBLE TWO'S: MASTERING THE ART OF SAYING NO

The terrible two's have considerable relevance for empowered parenting. During that stage of development, your child may start to say no to almost any request. This, of course, results in some frustration on your part. You have been doing your best to make the household and parenting tasks move along with some efficiency in the faint hope that you might get some time to yourself at the end of the evening.

"Go get your pj's on, it's almost bedtime."

"No. Don't wanna."

"I said go get your pj's on!"

"No."

"You do it now or I'll get your dad in here!"

"No!"

The child throws himself on the floor, screaming, kicking the floor and turning red. You feel powerless, overwhelmed and angry. Your child may get dragged kicking and screaming into the bedroom, in an effort to enforce the request to get ready for bed. Your child is seen as uncooperative. Worse yet, your child might then get labelled as a defiant problem child or even diagnosed with 'oppositional defiant disorder' in a movement towards pathologizing what is normal, albeit challenging, behavior. It is telling that in the present social mores, there is no corresponding 'over co-operational submissive disorder.' Eager obedience represents a much more serious problem than does defiance.

In empowered parenting, a key question is this:

What exactly is your child attempting to master in this particular situation?

An empowerment perspective regarding the defiance that manifests in the terrible twos is that your child may be attempting to master the skill of saying no to things that he doesn't want. This is an extremely important skill and one that every reasonable parent wants for their child as they grow and develop and encounter experiences not to their liking. If you want your children to be able to 'just say no' to drugs, they must first learn that they can say no and have that no respected.

A two year old is responding to the world from an extremely powerless position in relation to the events that unfold around her during the course of the day. For example, much bigger people may physically pick her up without warning and carry her off to some other location. She is told when to eat, when to play and when to go to bed and all these decisions may be made without her consultation or input. It is not surprising then, that the two year old would attempt to gain a sense of empowerment by practicing the skill of saying no. From this perspective, the parenting task is to help the child learn how to say no and to develop a real sense of having some power and impact over things.

Proactive parenting requires planning and forethought so that you are not merely reacting to the latest manifestation of the two-year-olds challenging behavior. You, as a proactive parent, may therefore start your day out by setting up a number of opportunities for your child to say no. This might involve asking your child several questions to which they may give no as a valid and accepted answer. Questions are phrased in such a way that 'no' is a possible response:

"You can brush your teeth with the red toothbrush or the blue one. Would you like to use the blue one?"

"Would you like me to pick you up and take you into the kitchen?"

The goal of posing these questions is that your child can then practice saying no to the things that she doesn't want. The no answer should be respected in a relaxed and comfortable fashion.

"Would you like me to pick you up and take you into the kitchen?"

"No!"

"OK, well I'm going to go into the kitchen to put the dishes away."

It is important to note that there is no trick or manipulation in these questions; you are simply providing your child with genuine examples of things to which she can say no and have her answer respected. That's empowering because she now has a real say in the things that happen to her.

Questions that are likely to be responded to with a yes are also posed, so that your child can learn to discriminate what she wants from what she doesn't want:

"Would you like me to pick you up and give you an airplane ride?"

"Do you want to have some ice cream?"

Empowered parenting is about change, development and growth. You take the time and effort to identify the developmental task with which your child is faced. Then, armed with that knowledge, you watch for and create a series of opportunities (developmental challenge windows) that allow for your child to practice and attain mastery of that challenge. You remain vigilant and prepared to use naturally occurring incidents as they occur, while also deliberately creating moments that allow for the practice of the relevant skill. This style of empowered parenting thus becomes spontaneously interwoven into the routine events of your day.

If your two-year-old can practice saying no repeatedly in situations where no is accepted as an answer, she will have a voice in her two-year-old world. She will experience the beginnings of empowerment by having a say in what happens to her. The interaction will become less emotional for all concerned and there will no longer be a need for a battle for control.

Over time, she will become more relaxed and comfortable in using that skill. Saying no to things that don't feel right will become a natural and well-integrated part of your child's skill set. As a result, she will be more resistant to peer pressure and to bullying as she gets older.

CHALLENGES IN TEEN-AGE YEARS

Empowered parenting is applicable across all ages and developmental stages. There are many situations that arise in the pre-adolescent and teen years that make for challenging opportunities to practice the art of empowered parenting.

A mother noticed that her adolescent daughter looked distressed when getting off the school bus. Concerned, she confronted her daughter as to why she was upset and her daughter broke into tears. She explained that she felt the school bus driver didn't like her. The bus driver would scowl at her when she got on or off the bus and never greeted her or spoke to her. The teen, being quite sensitive to the opinions of others, had developed a great deal of anxiety around being on the bus. Whenever she got on or off the bus she would pull her cap down over her face and avoid all eye contact with the bus driver. She was sure, though, that she could feel the bus driver's icy stare as she exited the steps. She was completely bewildered as to what she had done wrong and, worse, was becoming more and more afraid to get on the bus. The mother, on hearing this story, became furious and planned to confront the apparently rude bus driver and "take a strip off her."

I discussed with the mother how this situation might be an opportunity for empowered parenting. This would require being proactive rather than reactive, as in her plan to blast the bus driver. What did she think was the developmental challenge that her daughter was facing in this situation? How could she use this challenge to grow and become a more empowered person?

On reflection of these questions, the mother identified the issue as her daughter trying to deal with a difficult and rejecting person. She quickly saw the utility in helping her daughter master this scenario, as the situation was sure to present itself later in life.

This represents a shift in focus from reactive to proactive. Resolving the current situation pales in importance to developing the skills that will help her throughout her life. It's not about getting to a point where the problem is over and now you can go back to the way things were. It is about growth and change; it's about developing empowerment.

The mother encouraged her daughter to come up with a plan for how she might deal with the rejecting bus driver. With her mother's coaching and support, the daughter came up with following strategy: she would look the bus driver in the eye and greet her with a smile and a cheery hello, everyday, for the following week. She was, however, extremely reluctant to act on the plan, fully expecting that the school bus driver would reject her. In spite of her daughter's skepticism, her mother continued to encourage her in trying out the strategy.

Happily, the plan worked even better than either had expected. By the end of the week the bus driver was greeting her warmly and calling out her name with a huge smile every time she saw her. They started to engage in small talk and banter. Riding the bus became a welcome and pleasant experience and she began to feel that she had an adult looking out for her on the bus. She felt safer. She never did find out why the bus driver had been giving her the cold shoulder, but that became unimportant in light of her new relationship. More significantly, this young girl had the experience of mastering a difficult interpersonal situation and had developed valuable skills as a result. She learned that she was not helpless even in the face of seemingly inexplicable events. She learned that she could strategize in dealing with challenging situations and then carry out that plan in a systematic and persistent way. That's a lesson in proactivity. She discovered that she had options other than simply avoiding the situation and that she didn't have to be stuck with ongoing feelings of anxiety in the face of challenges.

It was not only the daughter who was changed by the experience; these events had a transformative impact on the mother as well. The mother felt that she now had skills for managing similar situations in the future. The way in which mother and daughter faced the challenge together resulted in far-reaching effects for parent and child. They both developed a sense of mastery from the situation: the mother in her parenting ability and the daughter in her ability to manage the feeling of disapproval from an adult.

What began as a confusing and negative situation ultimately became a positive opportunity for learning and growth for mother and daughter. Both are stronger for the experience. Contrast that with the likely outcome if the angry mother had, in fact, torn a strip off the bus driver in an attempt to protect her child from the difficult situations in the world.

One of the consequences of empowered parenting is that you develop a view of stressful life events as possibilities for growth and development, rather than as unfortunate obstacles that need to be avoided or endured. From the perspective of empowered parenting, life problems become opportunities for self-actualization.

Bibliography

American Psychiatric Association. (2013). *Diagnostic and statistical manual of mental disorders* (5th ed.) Washington, DC: American Psychiatric Publishing.

Alster, B. (2005). *Wisdom of Ancient Sumer.* Bethesda, MD, CDL Press.

Brown, D. P. (2006). *Pointing out the great way: The stages of meditation in the mahamudra tradition.* Boston: Wisdom Publications.

Covey, S. (2003). *The 7 Habits of Highly Effective People: Powerful Lessons in Personal Change.* New York, Fireside.

Csikszentmihalyi, M. (1990). *Flow: The Psychology of Optimal Experience.* New York, Harper Collins.

Csikszentmihalyi, M. (1997). *Finding Flow, The Psychology of Engagement with Everyday Life*, New York, HarperCollins Publishers, Inc.

Darwin, C. (2009). *The Autobiography of Charles Darwin.* New York, Classic Books International.

Gandhi, M.K. (1977). *An Autobiography, or The Story of My Experiments with Truth.* Ahmadabad, Navajivan Publishing House.

Goodman, F. & Nauwald, N. (2003). *Ecstatic Trance: New Ritual Body Postures.* Holland, Binkey Kok Publications.

Lake, J. H., & Spiegal, D. (2007). *Complementary and Alternative Treatments in Mental Health Care.* Washington, American Psychiatric Publishing.

Lederbogen, F., Kirsch, P., Haddad, L., Streit, F., Tost, H., Schuch, P., Wust, S., Pruesnner, J.C., Rietschel, M., Deuschle, M., & Myer-Lindenberger, A. (2011). City living and urban upbringing affect neural social stress processing in humans. *Nature, 474*, 498–501.

Meade, M. (2010). *Fate and Destiny: The Two Agreements of the Soul*. Seattle, Greenfire Press.

Milgram, S. (1975). *Obedience to Authority: The Experiment That Challenged Human Nature*. New York, Harper & Row.

Orlick, T. (2008). *In Pursuit of Excellence*. Illinois, Human Kinetics.

Pagels, E. (1981). *The Gnostic Gospels*. New York, Random House.

Rogers, C. R. (1957). The necessary and sufficient conditions of therapeutic personality change. Journal of Consulting Psychology, 21, 95-103.

Salter, A. (1949). *Conditioned Reflex Therapy*. London, Allen.

Sartre, J.P. (1956). *Being and Nothingness*. New York, Simon and Schuster.

Shakespeare, W. (1992). *Hamlet, Prince of Denmark*. New York, Washington Square Press.

Siegel, D. J. (1999). *The Developing Mind*. New York: Guilford Press.

Smith, R. (2007). *Cranial Electrotherapy Stimulation: It's First Fifty Years, Plus Three: A Monograph*. Oklahoma, Tate Publishing.

Tick, E. (2005). *War and the Soul*. Wheaton, Ill. Quest Books.

Welburn, K., Dagg., P., Coristine, M., & Pontefract, A. (2000). Schema change from twelve weeks of intensive group therapy. *Psychotherapy*, 37 (2): 189-195.

Zimbardo, P. (2007). *The Lucifer Effect: Understanding How Good People Turn Evil*. New York, Random House.

Appendix

EXAMPLES OF BEHAVIORAL GOALS

1. Cognitive Goal. Example: I will practice coaching myself in a positive and encouraging way 3 times per day. I will visualize myself succeeding once a day for 10 weeks.
2. Behavioral Goal. Example: I will speak in the group at least twice per session. I will take a bus ride for at least 20 minutes twice a week for 10 weeks.
3. Stress Management Goal: I will go to yoga once per week for next 10 weeks. I will give myself a quiet time to read 30 minutes per day, three times a week for 10 weeks.

CREATING A HIERARCHY FOR GRADED EXPOSURE
(Breaking Goals Into Manageable and Do-able Steps)

10
(Most Difficult)

9

8

7

6

5
(Moderate)

4

3

2

1
(Easy, I do it now)

Starting Goal: *(Set goal in the 3-5 difficulty range).*

MONITORING ANXIETY OVER 10 WEEKS

WEEK	AVERAGE RATING OF ANXIETY ON A SCALE OF 1 TO 10	NUMBER OF PANIC ATTACKS *(IF APPLICABLE)*
1		
2		
3		
4		
5		
6		
7		
8		
9		
10		

Rate your average level of anxiety over the past week on a scale of 1 to 10.

Base your rating on the following:

1 = not anxious at all
5 = moderately anxious
10 = most anxious I have ever been in my life

DWELLING ON THE POSITIVE

WEEK	ONE IMPORTANT THING I LEARNED TODAY
1	
2	
3	
4	
5	
6	
7	
8	
9	
10	

COGNITIVE-BEHAVIORAL SELF-MONITORING FORM
Identifying Anxiety-Related Thoughts, Images and Core Beliefs

Situation (just the facts):

_____

_____

_____

_____

Emotions:

_____

_____

_____

Thoughts:

_____

_____

_____

Positive Thoughts:

_____

_____

_____

_____

MY LIST OF ACTIVITIES
FOR PARASYMPATHETIC RELAXATION

1.

_____

2.

_____

3.

_____

4.

_____

5.

_____

6.

_____

7.

_____

8.

_____

9.

_____

10.

_____

Welburn Empathic Concern Scale

WECS

Check the response that describes you best

1 - Not true of me
2 - Seldom true of me
3 - Sometimes true of me
4 - Often true of me
5 - Completely true of me

#	Statement	1	2	3	4	5
1.	I can strongly feel what other people feel.	□	□	□	□	□
2.	I easily pick up on the feelings of others.	□	□	□	□	□
3.	I care about what happens to the people around me.	□	□	□	□	□
4.	I feel strongly when I see sad things on TV.	□	□	□	□	□
5.	I have strong emotional reactions when reading a good book.	□	□	□	□	□
6.	I can usually tell what my friends are feeling.	□	□	□	□	□
7.	I often put myself "in the other person's shoes."	□	□	□	□	□
8.	At times, I can feel what other people are feeling almost as strongly as they do.	□	□	□	□	□
9.	I can't bear to see animals suffer.	□	□	□	□	□
10.	It's easy for me to see the other person's point of view.	□	□	□	□	□
11.	I care a great deal about what happens to people.	□	□	□	□	□
12.	I'm very sensitive to the feelings of others.	□	□	□	□	□
13.	I am a compassionate person.	□	□	□	□	□
14.	At times I feel like I can take on the other person's feelings so much, it's like I've become them for a moment.	□	□	□	□	□
15.	It upsets me to see people suffer.	□	□	□	□	□
16.	I feel very emotional when I see people treated unfairly.	□	□	□	□	□
17.	I feel a sense of responsibility even towards people I don't know.	□	□	□	□	□
18.	Injustice bothers me a great deal.	□	□	□	□	□

Score

WECS – Welburn Empathic Concern Scale

(Scoring Sheet)

Name: File no.:   Date:

Score*	Percentiles Male	Percentiles Female	
90	99	99	
89	98	98	
88	97	96	
87	96	93	High
86	95	91	
85	95	88	
84	95	84	
83	95	81	
82	94	77	
81	93	74	
80	89	69	
79	87	66	
78	86	62	
77	81	58	
76	79	54	
75	76	50	
74	74	46	Average
73	72	43	
72	70	40	
71	68	35	
70	66	32	
69	63	30	
68	62	27	
67	58	25	
66	54	23	
65	50	19	
64	46	17	
63	42	16	
62	41	14	
61	39	13	
60	36	12	
59	34	10	
58	32	8	
57	31	7	
56	28	6	Low
55	25	4	
54	22	3	
53	21	3	
52	21	3	
51	20	3	
50	16	3	
<50			

*Score = sum of item scores

Score: _____ /90

Percentile: _____

Copyright: Dr. Ken Welburn
Ottawa Anxiety and Trauma Clinic, 202-2277 Riverside Dr., Ottawa ON K1H 7X6

Index

About the Author

Ken Welburn, Ph.D., C Psych

D r. Welburn is the Clinical Director of the Ottawa Anxiety & Trauma Clinic.

He is one of the pioneers of trauma treatment in Canada. He was involved in developing and teaching the first Canadian Psychiatric Association's trauma-related courses, both in PTSD and in Dissociative Disorders, in the early 1990's.

Dr. Welburn has practiced and taught cognitive-behavioral therapy, hypnosis, ego-state therapy and other trauma-related treatments over three decades.

In 2014, he developed an innovative trauma treatment: Juggling-Exposure Therapy (JET), a neuro-behavioral therapy using juggling to stimulate neural activity in order to overcome trauma-related startle reactions.

He co-chaired the Ottawa Annual Trauma conference since it's inception in 1990 in collaboration with world re-known experts in trauma.

He has lectured internationally on topics such as: trauma treatments; compassion fatigue; hypnosis; peak performance training in anxiety treatment; trauma and return to work; empathy, imagery and PTSD; police crisis work and trauma; PTSD in the military; PTSD and First Responders; integrating EMDR and ego-state therapy in the treatment of dissociation; and childhood trauma in the history of patients in emergency psychiatry.

www.ingramcontent.com/pod-product-compliance
Lightning Source LLC
Chambersburg PA
CBHW060836280326
41934CB00007B/811